everyday Phonics

Intervention Activities

Table of Contents

Using Everyday Phonics Intervention Activities

Current research identifies phonemic awareness and phonics as the essential skills for reading success.

- **Phonemic awareness** is the ability to notice, think about, and work with the individual sounds in spoken words. Before children learn to read print, they need to become aware of how the sounds in words work. They must understand that words are made up of speech sounds, or phonemes.

- **Phonics** instruction teaches children the relationships between the letters (graphemes) of written language and the individual sounds (phonemes) of spoken language. Children learn to use the relationships to read and write words. Knowing the relationships will help children recognize familiar words accurately and automatically, and "decode" new words.

Although some students master these skills easily during regular classroom instruction, many others need additional re-teaching opportunities to master these essential skills. The Everyday Phonics Intervention Activities series provides easy-to-use, five-day intervention units for Grades K–5. These units are structured around a research-based Model-Guide-Practice-Apply approach. You can use these activities in a variety of intervention models, including Response to Intervention (RTI).

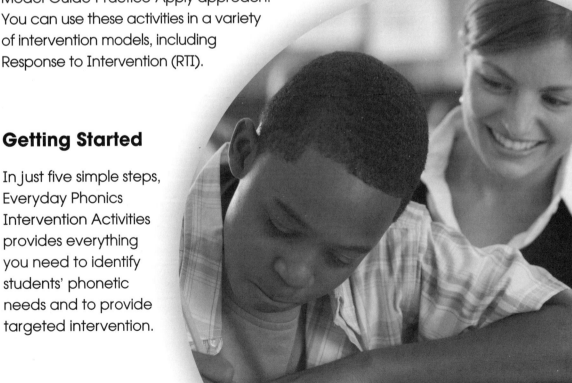

Getting Started

In just five simple steps, Everyday Phonics Intervention Activities provides everything you need to identify students' phonetic needs and to provide targeted intervention.

1. PRE-ASSESS to identify students' Phonemic Awareness and Phonics needs.

Use the pre-assessment on the CD-ROM to identify the skills your students need to master.

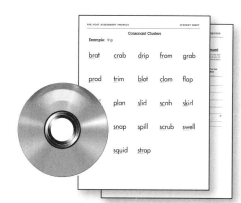

2. MODEL the skill.

Every five-day unit targets a specific phonetic element. On Day 1, use the teacher prompts and reproducible activity page to introduce and model the skill.

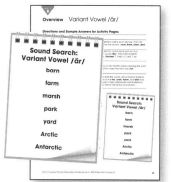

Day 1

3. GUIDE PRACTICE and APPLY.

Use the reproducible practice activities for Days 2, 3, and 4 to build students' understanding and skill-proficiency.

Day 2 Day 3 Day 4

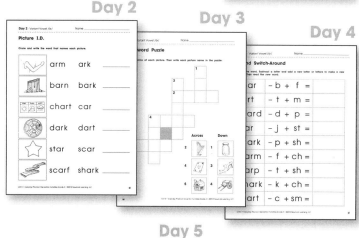

Day 5

4. MONITOR progress.

Administer the Day 5 reproducible assessment to monitor each student's progress and to make instructional decisions.

5. POST-ASSESS to document student progress.

Use the post-assessment on the CD-ROM to measure students' progress as a result of your interventions.

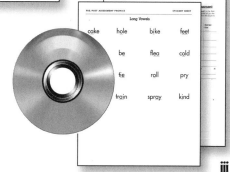

Standards-Based Phonemic Awareness & Phonics Skills in Everyday Intervention Activities

The Phonemic Awareness and Phonics skills found in the Everyday Intervention Activities series are introduced developmentally and spiral from one grade to the next. The chart below shows the skill areas addressed at each grade level in this series.

Everyday Phonics Intervention Activities Series Skills	K	1	2	3	4	5
Phonemic Awareness	✔	✔	✔	✔		
Letter Identification and Formation	✔	✔				
Sound/Symbol Relationships	✔	✔				
Short Vowels		✔				
Consonants		✔				
Long Vowels			✔	✔		
Blends			✔	✔		
Digraphs			✔	✔		
Variant Vowels			✔	✔		
CVCe Syllable Patterns			✔	✔	✔	✔
Closed Syllable Patterns				✔	✔	✔
Open Syllable Patterns				✔	✔	✔
r-Controlled Syllable Patterns				✔	✔	✔
Diphthongs				✔	✔	✔
Silent Letters				✔	✔	✔
Regular and Irregular Plurals				✔	✔	✔
Contractions					✔	✔
Prefixes or Suffixes					✔	✔
Compound Words					✔	✔
Comparatives						✔
Greek and Latin Roots						✔
Homographs and Homophones						✔
Word Origins						✔

Using Everyday Intervention for RTI

According to the National Center on Response to Intervention, RTI "integrates assessment and intervention within a multi-level prevention system to maximize student achievement and to reduce behavior problems." This model of instruction and assessment allows schools to identify at-risk students, monitor their progress, provide research-proven interventions, and "adjust the intensity and nature of those interventions depending on a student's responsiveness."

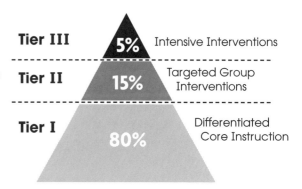

RTI models vary from district to district, but the most prevalent model is a three-tiered approach to instruction and assessment.

The Three Tiers of RTI	Using Everyday Intervention Activities
Tier I: Differentiated Core Instruction • Designed for all students • Preventive, proactive, standards-aligned instruction • Whole- and small-group differentiated instruction • Ninety-minute, daily core reading instruction in the five essential skill areas: phonics, phonemic awareness, comprehension, vocabulary, fluency	• Use whole-group comprehension mini-lessons to introduce and guide practice with comprehension strategies that all students need to learn. • Use any or all of the units in the order that supports your core instructional program.
Tier II: Targeted Group Interventions • For at-risk students • Provide thirty minutes of daily instruction beyond the ninety-minute Tier I core reading instruction • Instruction is conducted in small groups of three to five students with similar needs	• Select units based on your students' areas of need (the pre-assessment can help you identify these). • Use the units as week-long, small-group mini-lessons.
Tier III: Intensive Interventions • For high-risk students experiencing considerable difficulty in reading • Provide up to sixty minutes of additional intensive intervention each day in addition to the ninety-minute Tier I core reading instruction • More intense and explicit instruction • Instruction conducted individually or with smaller groups of one to three students with similar needs	• Select units based on your students' areas of need. • Use the units as one component of an intensive comprehension intervention program.

Overview CVCe Long Vowel Review

Directions and Sample Answers for Activity Pages

Day 1	See "Model the Skill" below.
Day 2	Read aloud the title and directions. Ask students to cut out the pictures and sort them by vowel sound. (**cake:** skates, grapes, plane. **bike:** slide, kite, mice. **cone:** globe, phone, note.)
Day 3	Read aloud the title and directions. Invite students to name each picture. Then help students unscramble the letters to spell each word.
Day 4	Read aloud the title and directions. Invite students to name each picture. Remind them to listen closely to the middle vowel sound. Then help students fill in the missing letters.
Day 5	Pronounce the following words slowly. Allow time after each word for students to write the word: **take, code, pine, gave, joke, side, ripe, same, vote.** Afterward, meet individually with students to discuss their results. Use the Grade 2 Phonics RTI book as a resource for students who are still struggling with long vowel sounds.

Model the Skill

◆ Hand out the Day 1 activity page.

◆ **Say:** *Today we are going to blend words that have a vowel followed by a consonant and a final **e**. This pattern tells us that the word has a long vowel sound. We will blend the sounds to read words. Let's look at the first word. Put your finger under the letter **r** at the beginning of the word and say the sounds aloud with me, moving your finger as we reach each letter sound.* Model how to blend the sounds. Put your finger under each letter as you extend the sound that each letter stands for. **Say: /r/ /ā/ /k/.** Students follow your lead, running their fingers under each letter as you blend them.

◆ **Say:** *What picture shows the word we just read? That's right. We read the word **rake**. Now draw a line from the word **rake** to the picture of a rake.* Allow students a moment to draw a line connecting the word to the picture.

◆ Have students blend the remaining words by making sure they run their fingers under the letters as they blend the sounds with you. Remind them that the pattern of vowel/consonant/final **e** means that the word has a long vowel sound. Allow time after each word for students to locate and draw a line to the correct picture.

◆ Write the following incomplete words on the board: __ **a__e**; __ **i__ e**; and __**o__e**. Pair students and have them invent a nonsense word for each pattern, such as **zake**, **vife**, and **loje**.

CVCe
Long Vowels

rake
kite
rose
tape
pole
cave
dime
bowl
dive

Blend, Read, and Match

Read each word. Then draw a line to the matching picture.

rake

kite

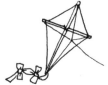

rose

tape

pole

cave

dime

bone

dive

Name _____

Vowel Sound Sort

Cut out the pictures. Sort them in columns by the long vowel sounds.

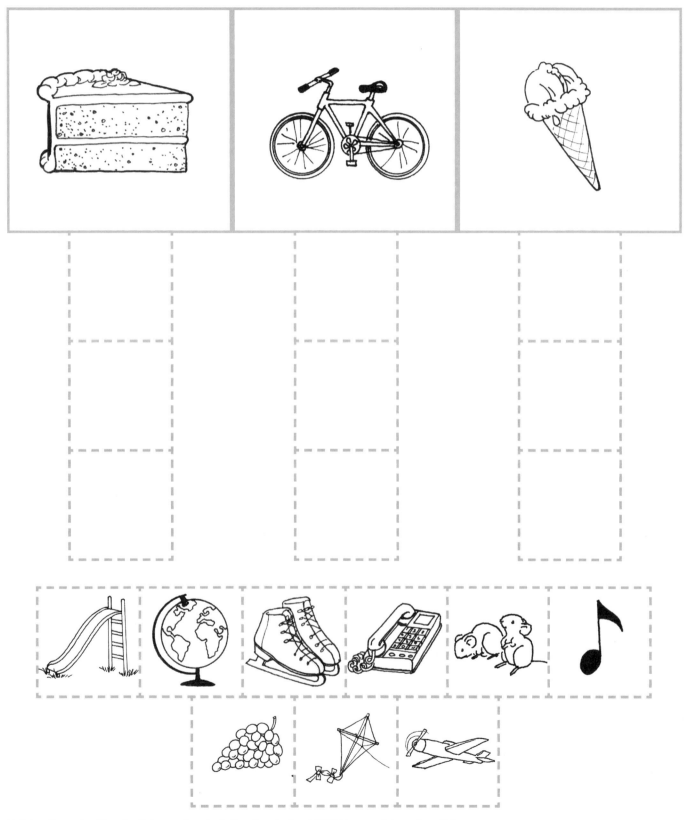

Word Scramble

Name the pictures. Then unscramble the letters to spell the words.

 oreb   __ __ __ __

 eimt   __ __ __ __

 kcea   __ __ __ __

 evni   __ __ __ __

 ehlo   __ __ __ __

 geta   __ __ __ __

 eopr   __ __ __ __

 einn   __ __ __ __

 veaw   __ __ __ __

Unit 1 • Everyday Phonics Intervention Activities Grade 3 • ©2010 Newmark Learning, LLC

Missing Letters

Name the pictures. Listen to the middle vowel sounds. Then write the missing letters on the lines.

 h __ m __

 p __ p __

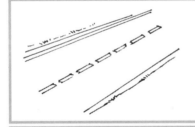 l __ n __

 h __ v __

 c __ n __

 r __ p __

Assessment

Listen to your teacher say each word. Write the words on the lines.

1. _____

2. _____

3. _____

4. _____

5. _____

6. _____

7. _____

8. _____

9. _____

Overview   Long Vowel Digraphs Review

Directions and Sample Answers for Activity Pages

Day 1	See "Model the Skill" below.
Day 2	Read aloud the title and directions. Invite students to name each picture clue. Tell them that each word has a long **a** sound. Have students complete the crossword. (**Across:** 3. train; 4. hay. **Down:** 1. braid; 2. snail; 3. tray.)
Day 3	Read aloud the title and directions. Model how to do the first one by reading the word **lie**. Then show how to take away **l** and add **t** to make the new word **tie**.
Day 4	Read aloud the title and directions. Invite students to read the sentences and circle one or more words in each sentence with a long **o** sound. Have them write the letters that make /ō/. (**snow/ow; Joan/oa; goat/oa; toad/oa; row/ow; boat/oa; bow/ow**)
Day 5	Read the directions aloud. Allow time for students to complete the first task. Pronounce the following words slowly. Allow time after each word for students to write the word: **wait**, **say**, **tight**, **fright**, **slow**, and **road**. Afterward, meet individually with students to discuss their results. Use the Grade 2 Phonics RTI book as a resource for students who are still struggling with long vowel digraphs.

Model the Skill

◆ Hand out the Day 1 activity page.

◆ **Say:** *Today you are going to blend words that have long vowel digraphs. You will blend the sounds to read words. Let's look at the first word. Put your finger under the letter **s** at the beginning of the word and say the sounds aloud with me, moving your finger as we reach each letter sound.* Model how to blend the sounds. Put your finger under each letter as you extend the sound that each letter stands for. **Say:** */s/ /ē/ /l/.* Students follow your lead, running their fingers under each letter as you blend them.

◆ **Say:** *What picture shows the word we just read? That's right. We read the word **seal**. Now draw a line from the word **seal** to the picture of a seal.* Allow students a moment to draw a line connecting the word to the picture.

◆ Have students blend the remaining words with long **e** digraphs by making sure they run their fingers under the letters as they blend the sounds with you. Allow time after each word for students to locate and draw a line to the correct picture.

◆ Put ā, ō, ē, and ī on index cards in a pocket chart. Distribute words on index cards with the different long vowel digraphs, including **high**, **pie**, **bean**, **green**, **show**, **load**, **bay**, and **gain**. Ask students to read the words and place them under the correct long vowel.

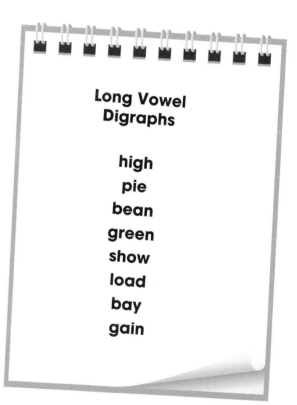

Long Vowel Digraphs

high
pie
bean
green
show
load
bay
gain

Blend, Read, and Match

Read each word. Then draw a line to the matching picture.

seal

pea

wheel

tea

beak

bee

meat

three

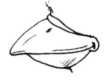

Long *a* Crossword Puzzle

Say the name of each picture. Then write each picture name in the puzzle.

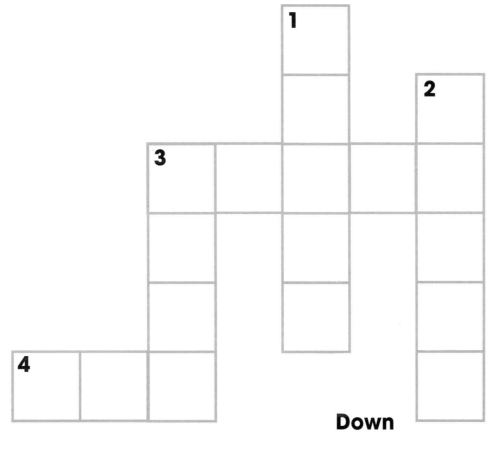

Down

Across

3

4

2

3

Make a Word

Read the word. Subtract a letter or letters and add a new letter or letters to make a new word with a long *i* sound. Then read the new word.

lie	– l + t =	
fight	– f + r =	
cried	– cr + fr =	
thigh	– th + s =	
might	– m + n =	
flies	– fl + sp =	

 Unit 2 • Everyday Phonics Intervention Activities Grade 3 • ©2010 Newmark Learning, LLC

Long *o* Hunt

Find one or more words in each sentence that makes a long *o* sound. Circle the words and write the letters that stand for the long *o* sound on the lines.

 I love snow.   _____

 Joan has a goat.   _____

 I see a toad!   _____

 Row the boat.   _____

 Her bow is big.   _____

Assessment

Match words in the columns that have the same long vowel sound.

wait   heel

bean   bye

low   pay

high   soak

Listen to your teacher say each word. Write the words on the lines.

1. _____   4. _____

2. _____   5. _____

3. _____   6. _____

Overview   Initial Blend Review

Directions and Sample Answers for Activity Pages

Day 1	See "Model the Skill" below.
Day 2	Read aloud the title and directions. Have students cut out each small picture and paste it under the big picture that begins with the same blend. (**skis/skates; frog/fruit; snake/snail; slide/sled; broom/bridge; cloud/clock**)
Day 3	Read aloud the title and directions. Have students write the blends to make rhyming words. Then have them draw what they wrote. (**flag, frog, swing, skip**)
Day 4	Read aloud the title and directions. Invite students to name each picture. Then have them fill in the missing letters.
Day 5	Pronounce the following words slowly. Allow time after each word for students to write the word: **blot, clay, flip, glad, plan, slab, skin, smog, snip, span, stop, swam, brat, crop, drip, from, grin,** and **prop**. Afterward, meet individually with students to discuss their results. Use the Grade 2 Phonics RTI book as a resource for students who are still struggling with initial blends.

Model the Skill

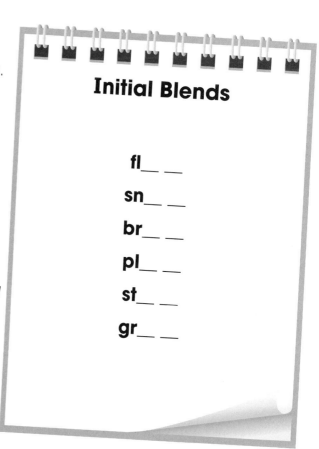

Initial Blends

fl__ __

sn__ __

br__ __

pl__ __

st__ __

gr__ __

◆ Hand out the Day 1 activity page.

◆ Write the words **clap**, **drab**, **snap** in a row on the board. Point out that each word starts with a different type of blend. Remind students that a blend is two or three letters that stand for a blended sound. Circle each blend as you read it and tell students what blend family each belongs to (**l**-family, **r**-family, or **s**-family).

◆ Point to the word **flag** at the top of the activity page. Model sounding out the word, blending each sound as you run your finger under the letters: **/fl/ /a/ /g/**. Then say the whole word. Point out that the words starts with an **l**-family blend.

◆ **Say:** *What picture shows the word we just read? That's right. We read the word* **flag.** *Draw a line from the word* **flag** *to the picture of a flag.* Allow students a moment to draw a line connecting the word to the picture.

◆ Have students blend the remaining words. Allow time after each word for students to locate and draw a line to the correct picture.

◆ Write the following incomplete words on the board: **fl__ __; sn__ __; br__ __; pl__ __; st__ __; gr__ __.** Pair students and have them build a word starting with each blend.

Name _____

Blend, Read, and Match

Read each word. Then draw a line to the matching picture.

flag

swan

crab

plane

star

drum

Name _____

Sound Match

Cut out each small picture and paste it under the big picture that begins with the same blend.

Name _____

Rhyming Words

Review the blends at the bottom. Write the blends to make rhyming words. Then draw a picture of each word.

hag

___ ag

log

___ ___ og

ring

___ ___ ing

rip

___ ___ ip

| sw | fl | sk | fr |

 Unit 3 • Everyday Phonics Intervention Activities Grade 3 • ©2010 Newmark Learning, LLC

Missing Letters

Name the pictures. Listen to the initial blend sounds. Then write the missing letters on the lines.

___ ___ ib

___ ___ ow

___ ___ ates

___ ___ ant

___ ___ ir

___ ___ ow

___ ___ ot

___ ___ ush

Name _____

Assessment

Listen to your teacher say each word. Write the words on the lines.

1. _____

2. _____

3. _____

4. _____

5. _____

6. _____

7. _____

8. _____

9. _____

10. _____

11. _____

12. _____

13. _____

14. _____

15. _____

16. _____

17. _____

18. _____

Overview Final Blend Review

Directions and Sample Answers for Activity Pages

Day 1	See "Model the Skill" below.
Day 2	Read aloud the title and directions. Have students cut out each small picture and paste it under the big picture that ends with the same blend. (**cast/vest; wink/link; wand/pond; tent/paint; stump/jump**)
Day 3	Read aloud the title and directions. Model how to do the first one by reading the word **rest**. Then show how to take away **r** and add **b** to make the new word **best**.
Day 4	Read aloud the title and directions. Invite students to name each picture. Then have them fill in the missing letters.
Day 5	Pronounce the following words slowly. Allow time after each word for students to write the word: **left**, **gulp**, **tilt**, **bump**, **stink**, **want**, and **dust**. Afterward, meet individually with students to discuss their results. Use the Grade 2 Phonics RTI book as a resource for students who are still struggling with final blends.

Model the Skill

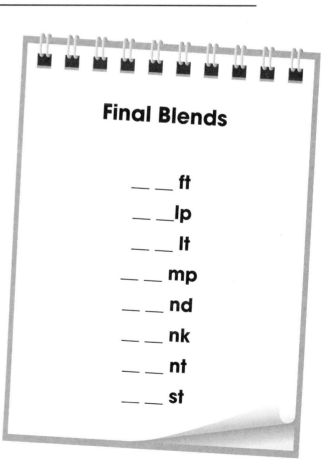

Final Blends

__ __ ft

__ __lp

__ __ lt

__ __ mp

__ __ nd

__ __ nk

__ __ nt

__ __ st

◆ Hand out the Day 1 activity page.

◆ Write the words **bent, clunk, fond, jump, lift, felt, help,** and **past** in a row on the board. Point out that each word ends with a different type of blend. Remind students that a blend is two or three letters that stand for a blended sound. Circle each final blend as you read it and tell students what blend family each word belongs to (**nt, nk, nd, mp, ft, lt, lp,** or **st**).

◆ Point to the word **belt** at the top of the activity page. Model sounding out the word, blending each sound as you run your finger under the letters: **/b/ /e/ /l/ /t/**. Then say the whole word. Point out that the word ends with a two-letter blend.

◆ **Say:** *What picture shows the word we just read? That's right. We read the word **belt**. Now draw a line from the word **belt** to the picture of a belt.* Allow students a moment to draw a line connecting the word to the picture.

◆ Have students blend the remaining words. Allow time after each word for students to locate and draw a line to the correct picture.

◆ Write the following final two-letter blends on the board with lines preceding them: __ __ **ft**; __ __**lp**; __ __ **lt**; __ __ **mp**; __ __ **nd**; __ __ **nk**; __ __ **nt**; __ __ **st**. Pair students and have them build a word ending with each blend.

Blend, Read, and Match

Read each word. Then draw a line to the matching picture.

belt

stamp

gift

hand

skunk

ant

nest

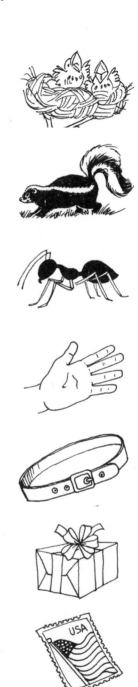

Sound Match

Cut out each small picture and paste it under the big picture that ends with the same blend.

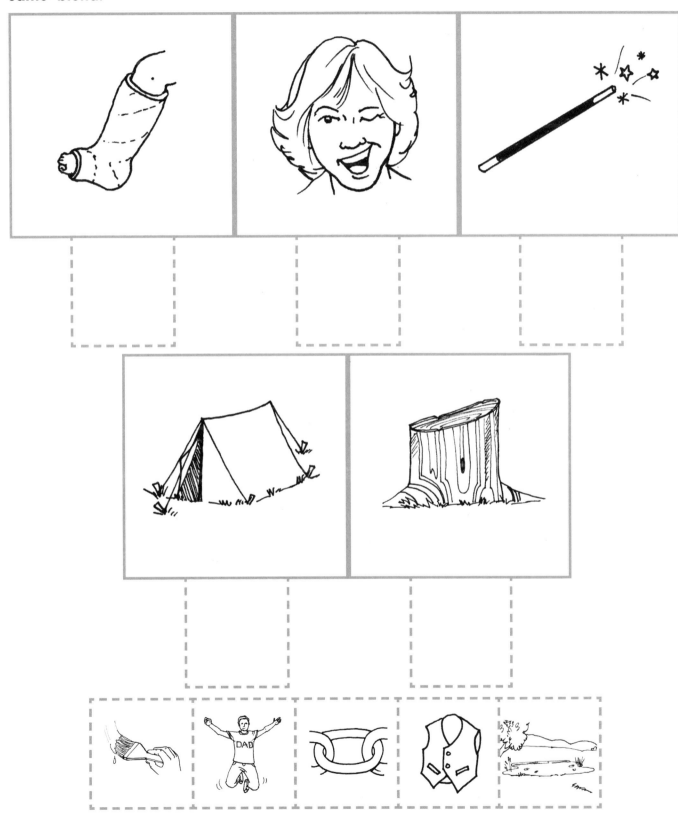

Blend Math

Solve each word equation and write the new words on the lines.

rest	– r + b =	
bent	– b + r =	
lump	– l + p =	
craft	– cr + dr =	
help	– h + y =	
felt	– f + m =	
mink	– m + p =	
grand	– gr + st =	

Missing Letters

Name the pictures. Listen to the final blend sounds. Then write the missing blends on the lines.

 li ___ ___

  sa ___ ___

 chi ___ ___

 ha ___ ___

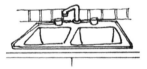 si ___ ___

 de ___ ___

 ne ___ ___

Name _____

Assessment

Listen to your teacher say each word. Write the words on the lines.

1. _____

2. _____

3. _____

4. _____

5. _____

6. _____

7. _____

Overview Consonant Digraphs ch, sh Review

Directions and Sample Answers for Activity Pages

Day 1	See "Model the Skill" below.
Day 2	Read aloud the title and directions. Have students cut out each picture and paste it in the box that has a picture with the same digraph in the same position. (**shell/shark; sandwich/couch; chick/chair; brush/leash**)
Day 3	Read aloud the title and directions. Have students write the two words in each set that begin or end with the same digraph. (**wish/gush; chew/chest; lunch/inch; shop/shape; crash/crush; sketch/scratch**)
Day 4	Read aloud the title and directions. Invite students to name each picture. Then have them fill in the missing digraph.
Day 5	Pronounce the following words slowly. Allow time after each word for students to write the word: **shut, cash, chat,** and **ranch**. Afterward, meet individually with students to discuss their results. Use the Grade 2 Phonics RTI book as a resource for students who are still struggling with consonant digraphs **ch** and **sh**.

Model the Skill

◆ Hand out the Day 1 activity page.

◆ Write the words **chase, rich, shape,** and **rush** in a row on the board. Point out that each word either begins or ends with a consonant digraph. Remind students that a digraph is two letters combined to make one sound. Circle each digraph as you read it (**ch, sh**).

◆ Point to the **fish** at the top of the activity page. Model sounding out the word, blending each sound as you run your finger under the letters: **/f/ /i/ /sh/**. Then say the whole word. Point out that the word ends with the **sh** digraph. Have students write the letters **sh** on the line after the picture to show where in the word they hear the digraph.

◆ Have students blend the remaining words. Allow time after each word for students to locate where the digraph occurs and write it on the appropriate line.

◆ Write the following incomplete words on the board: **ch __ __; sh__ __; __ __ ch; __ __ sh**. Pair students and have them build a word that starts or ends with the digraph **ch** or **sh**.

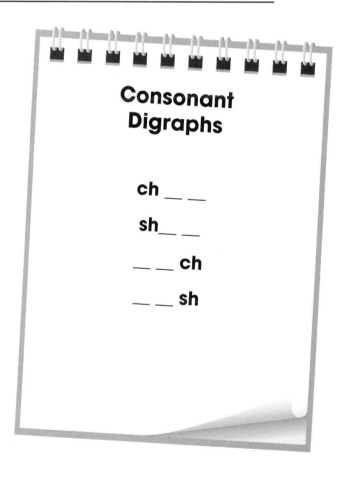

Consonant Digraphs

ch __ __

sh__ __

__ __ ch

__ __ sh

Where's the Digraph?

Look at each picture. Say the word aloud. Then write the sound you hear at the beginning or at the end of the word.

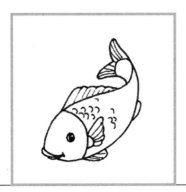

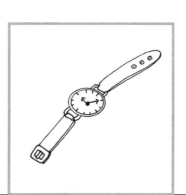

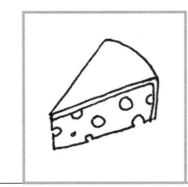

Picture Sort

Cut out each picture and paste it in the box that has a picture with the digraph *ch* or *sh* in the same position.

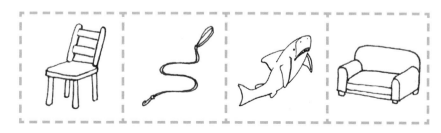

Alike and Different

Write the two words in each set that begin or end with the same digraph.

wish   gush   gum

_____

_____

shop   shape   stop

_____

_____

chew   cow   chest

_____

_____

crash   crack   crush

_____

_____

luck   lunch   inch

_____

_____

skate   sketch   scratch

_____

_____

Missing Letters

Name the pictures. Listen to the consonant digraphs at the beginning or the end of the words. Then write the missing letters on the lines.

     __ __ ip

   ben __ __

     bu __ __

   __ __ in

     __ __ irt

     pea __ __

Assessment

Listen to your teacher say each word. Write the words on the lines.

1. _____

2. _____

3. _____

4. _____

Overview   Consonant Digraphs
th, wh, ng, ck Review

Directions and Sample Answers for Activity Pages

Day 1	See "Model the Skill" below.
Day 2	Read aloud the title and directions. Have students cut out each small picture and paste it under the big picture that begins or ends with the same blend. (**whistle/whale; tooth/mouth; king/sing; lock/neck; three/thermometer**)
Day 3	Read aloud the title and directions. Model how to do the first one by reading the word **sink**. Then show how to take away **s** and add **th** to make the new word **think**.
Day 4	Read aloud the title and directions. Invite students to name each picture. Then have them fill in the missing digraph.
Day 5	Pronounce the following words slowly. Allow time after each word for students to write the word: **with, when, bring, deck,** and **that**. Afterward, meet individually with students to discuss their results. Use the Grade 2 Phonics RTI book as a resource for students who are still struggling with consonant digraphs **th, wh, ng,** and **ck**.

Model the Skill

◆ Hand out the Day 1 activity page.

◆ Write the words **luck, cloth, when,** and **hang** in a row on the board. Point out that each word has a consonant digraph at its beginning or end. Remind students that a digraph is two letters combined to make one sound. Circle each digraph as you read it (**ck, th, wh, ng**).

◆ Point to the word **sock** at the top of the activity page. Model sounding out the word, blending each sound as you run your finger under the letters: **/s/ /o/ /k/**. Remind students that the letters **c** and **k** together stand for the final **/k/** sound. Point out that the word **sock** ends with a consonant digraph.

◆ **Say:** *What picture shows the word we just read? That's right. We read the word **sock**. Now draw a line from the word **sock** to the picture of a sock.* Allow students a moment to draw a line connecting the word to the picture.

◆ Have students blend the remaining words. Allow time after each word for students to locate and draw a line to the correct picture.

◆ Write the following incomplete words on the board: __ __ **ck;** **th**__ __; __ __ **th; wh**__ __; __ __ **ng**. Pair students and have them build a word that starts or ends with the digraphs.

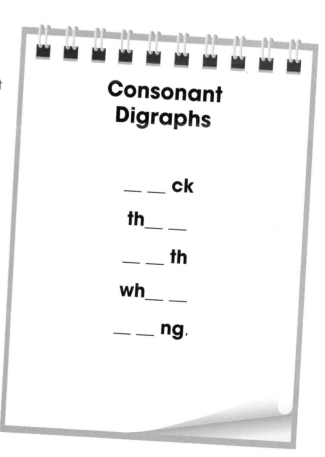

**Consonant
Digraphs**

__ __ **ck**

th__ __

__ __ **th**

wh__ __

__ __ **ng**.

Blend, Read, and Match

Read each word. Then draw a line to the matching picture.

sock

bath

clock

ring

wheel

thumb

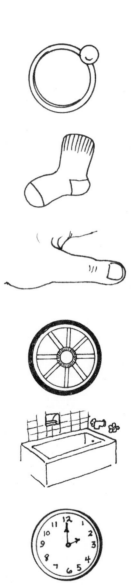

Sound Match

Cut out each small picture and paste it under the big picture that begins or ends with the same digraph.

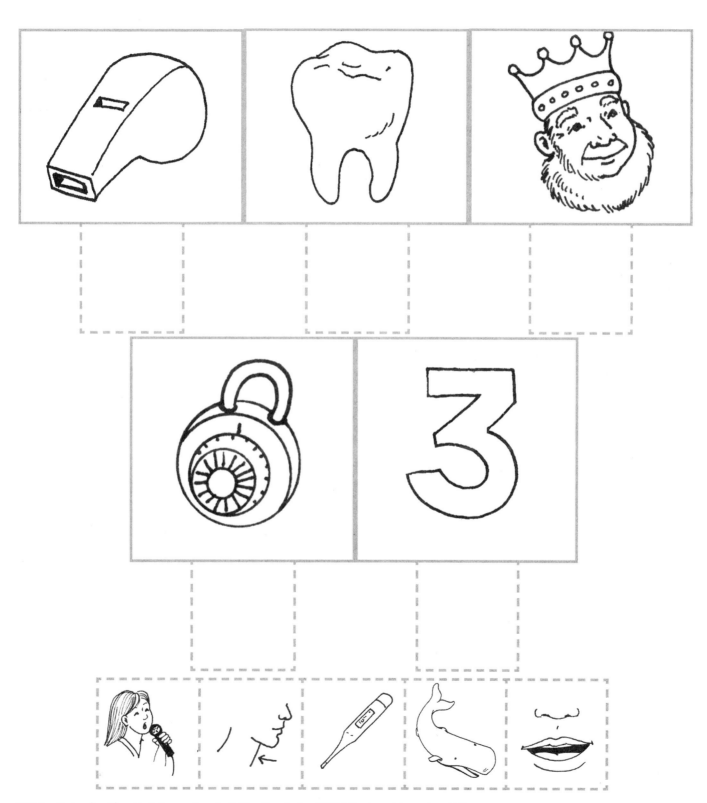

Make a Word

Solve each word equation and write the new word on the line.

sink	– s + th =	
lid	– d + ck =	
sank	– s + th =	
hat	– t + ng =	
men	– m + wh =	

    Unit 6 • Everyday Phonics Intervention Activities Grade 3 • ©2010 Newmark Learning, LLC

Missing Letters

Name the pictures. Listen to the consonant digraphs at the beginning or the end of the words. Then write the missing letters on the lines.

chi __ __

__ __ row

swi __ __

__ __ isk

nor __ __

Assessment

Listen to your teacher say each word. Write the words on the lines.

1. _____

2. _____

3. _____

4. _____

5. _____

Overview Initial Three-Letter Blends Review

Directions and Sample Answers for Activity Pages

Day 1	See "Model the Skill" below.
Day 2	Read aloud the title and directions. Have students write the three-letter blends to make rhyming words. Then have them draw what they wrote. (**scrub, squish, strum, spray, split**)
Day 3	Read aloud the title and directions. Model how to do the first one by reading the word **tape**. Then show how to take away **t** and add **scr** to make the new word **scrape**.
Day 4	Read aloud the title and directions. Invite students to write the three-letter blend that begins each word. (**scr, spl, squ, str, spr**)
Day 5	Pronounce the following words slowly. Allow time after each word for students to write the word: **scrub**, **squirt**, **strap**, **sprint**, and **splint**. Afterward, meet individually with students to discuss their results. Use the Grade 2 Phonics RTI book as a resource for students who are still struggling with initial three-letter blends.

Model the Skill

◆ Hand out the Day 1 activity page.

◆ Write the words **scratch, splice, sprint, stretch,** and **squat** in a row on the board. Point out that each word starts with a three-letter blend. Remind students that a blend is a combination of two or three letters that stand for a blended sound. Circle each blend as you read it (**scr, spl, spr, str, squ**).

◆ Point to the word **string** at the top of the activity page. Model sounding out the word, blending each sound as you run your finger under the letters: **/str/ /i/ /ng/**. Then say the whole word. Point out that the words starts with a three-letter blend.

◆ **Say:** *What picture shows the word we just read? That's right. We read the word* **string**. *Now draw a line from the word* **string** *to the picture of string.* Allow students a moment to draw a line connecting the word to the picture.

◆ Have students blend the remaining words. Allow time after each word for students to locate and draw a line to the correct picture.

◆ Pair students and have them think of words starting with each of the following three-letter blends: **scr, spr, spl, str, squ**.

Initial Three-letter Blends

scr

spr

spl

str

squ

Blend, Read, and Match

Read each word. Then draw a line to the matching picture.

string

square

splash

screw

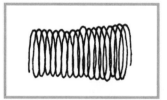

spring

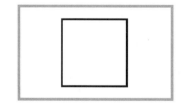

Rhyming Words

Review the three-letter blends at the bottom. Write the blends to make rhyming words. Then draw a picture of each word.

cub

___ ___ ___ ub

dish

___ ___ ___ ish

drum

___ ___ ___ um

tray

___ ___ ___ ay

hit

___ ___ ___ it

| spr | str | spl | scr | squ |

Make a Word

Read the word. Subtract the first letter in the word, add a three-letter blend, and make a new word. Then read the new word.

tape – t + scr = _____

lid – l + squ = _____

wide – w + str = _____

main – m + spr = _____

hint – h + spl = _____

Name That Blend

Name the pictures. Then write the three-letter blend that begins each picture.

_____

_____

_____

_____

_____

Assessment

Listen to your teacher say each word. Write the words on the lines.

1. _____

2. _____

3. _____

4. _____

5. _____

Overview   Variant Vowel /är/

Directions and Sample Answers for Activity Pages

Day 1	See "Model the Skill" below.
Day 2	Read aloud the title and directions. Invite students to name each picture. Then ask students to circle and write the word that names the picture. (**arm, bark, chart, dart, star, scarf**)
Day 3	Read aloud the title and directions. Invite students to name each picture clue, explaining that each one includes the variant vowel **/är/**. Then help students complete the crossword by filling in the words. (**Across:** 3. harp; 4. card; 5. jar. **Down:** 1. barn; 2. shark; 4. cart.)
Day 4	Read aloud the title and directions. Model how to do the first one by reading the word **bar**. Then show how to take away **b** and add **f** to make the new word **far**.
Day 5	Read the directions aloud and have students read the words. Allow time for students to complete the first task. Then pronounce the words **tar, arch, harm**, and **start** and ask students to write them on the lines. Afterward, meet individually with students to discuss their results. Use their responses to plan further instruction and review.

Model the Skill

◆ Hand out the Day 1 activity page and crayons.

◆ **Say:** *The dogs bark. What vowel sound do you hear in the word* **bark***? Listen again:* **/b/ /är/ /k/***. The vowel sound is not long or short. It is a different vowel sound. When the letter* **a** *is followed by the letter* **r***, the* **a** *makes the vowel sound* **/är/** *as in* **bark***.*

◆ Ask students to look at the picture of the farm. Write **farm** on the board. **Say:** *Look at the word* **farm***. Say the word with me:* **farm***. Listen as I say it slowly:* **/f/ /är/ /m/***. The vowel sound in* **farm** *is* **/är/***. The letters* **a** *and* **r** *stand for the* **/är/** *sound.*

◆ Help students find and color the other pictures that make the **/är/** sound. Write the words on the board as you find them: **barn, car, farmer**, and **cart**. Read each word slowly, circling the **ar** as you say **/är/**.

◆ Point out places that have the variant vowel **/är/** sound in their name. Write a few on chart paper and read aloud the words.

**Sound Search:
Variant Vowel /är/**

barn

farm

marsh

park

yard

Arctic

Antarctic

Name _____

At the Farm

Color the pictures that have the /ar/ sound like _farm_.

Unit 8 • Everyday Phonics Intervention Activities Grade 3 • ©2010 Newmark Learning, LLC

Picture I.D.

Circle and write the word that names each picture.

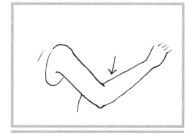   arm   ark

   barn   bark

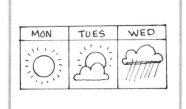   chart   car

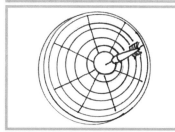   dark   dart

   star   scar _____

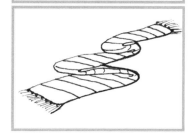   scarf   shark _____

Crossword Puzzle

Say the name of each picture. Then write each picture name in the puzzle.

Across

2

4

5

Down

1

3

4

Unit 8 • Everyday Phonics Intervention Activities Grade 3 • ©2010 Newmark Learning, LLC

Sound Switch-Around

Read the word. Subtract a letter and add a new letter or letters to make a new word. Then read the new word.

bar	– b + f =	
art	– t + m =	
hard	– d + p =	
jar	– j + st =	
park	– p + sh =	
farm	– f + ch =	
tarp	– t + sh =	
mark	– k + ch =	
cart	– c + sm =	
tar	– t + sc =	

Name _____

Assessment

Read the words. Circle the ones that have the same vowel sound as *car.*

hard	game
cake	garden
scar	play
mark	far
rat	part

Listen to your teacher say each word. Write the words on the lines.

1. _____

2. _____

3. _____

4. _____

Overview Variant Vowel /ûr/

Directions and Sample Answers for Activity Pages

Day 1	See "Model the Skill" below.
Day 2	Read aloud the title and directions. Invite students to name each picture. Then ask students to circle the pictures that have the same vowel sound as the word **turn**. (**purse, thirty, turtle, nurse, shirt, girl**)
Day 3	Read aloud the title and directions. Have students read the three words in each set, and write the two that have the vowel sound **/ûr/**. (**chirp, curb; her, hurt; burn/birth; fern, fir; nurse, nerve; surf, stir; turn, third**)
Day 4	Read aloud the title and directions. Model how to do the first one by reading the word **sir**. Then show how to take away **s** and add **f** to make the new word **fir**.
Day 5	Read the directions aloud and have students read the words. Allow time for students to complete the first task. Then pronounce the words **burst**, **first**, and **verb** and ask students to write them on the lines. Afterward, meet individually with students to discuss their results. Use their responses to plan further instruction and review.

Model the Skill

◆ Hand out the Day 1 activity page and crayons.

◆ **Say:** *Her party is today. What vowel sound do you hear in the word* **her**? *Listen again:* **/h/ /ûr/**. *The vowel sound is not long or short. It is a different vowel sound. When* **e**, **i**, *or* **u** *is followed by* **r**, *the* **e**, **i**, *or* **u** *makes the* **/ûr/** *sound, as in* **her**.

◆ Ask students to look at the picture. Point out that the girl has a curl in her hair. Write **curl** on the board. **Say:** *Look at the word* **curl**. *Say the word with me:* **curl**. *Listen as I say it slowly:* **/k/ /ûr/ /l/**. *The vowel sound in* **curl** *is* **/ûr/**. *The letters* **u** *and* **r** *stand for the* **/ûr/** *sound.* Have students color in the girl's curls.

◆ Help students find and color the other pictures that make the **/ûr/** sound. Write the words on the board as you find them: **girl, fur, birthday cake,** and **water**. Read each word slowly, circling the letters **ir, ur,** and **er**. Point out actions that have the variant vowel **/ûr/** sound. Write a few on chart paper and read aloud the words.

Sound Search:
Variant Vowel /ûr/

turn

surf

twirl

swirl

merge

swerve

Birthday Party

Color the parts of the picture that have the /ur/ sound like *purr*.

Unit 9 • Everyday Phonics Intervention Activities Grade 3 • ©2010 Newmark Learning, LLC

Name _____

Sound Search

Circle the pictures that have the same vowel sound as the word *turn*.

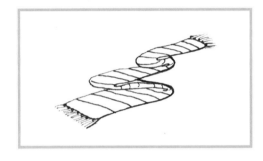

Name _____

Which Are Alike?

Write the two words in each set that have the vowel sound /ûr/.

chirp curb cub

_____

_____

nurse nerve north

_____

_____

hair her hurt

_____

_____

surf scarf stir

_____

_____

burn bun birth

_____

_____

tree turn third

_____

_____

far fern fir

_____

_____

Make a Word

Read the word. Subtract a letter or letters and add a new letter or letters to make a new word. Then read the new word.

sir	– s + f =	
turn	– t + b =	
nerve	– n + s =	
girl	– g + tw =	
curl	– c + h =	
clerk	– cl + j =	
shirt	– sh + sk =	
spur	– sp + f =	

Assessment

Read the words. Circle the ones that have the same vowel sound as _fern_.

perk	barn
fun	curb
clerk	blur
birth	rent
firm	dirt
run	

Listen to your teacher say each word. Write the words on the lines.

1. _____

2. _____

3. _____

Overview Variant Vowel /ôr/

Directions and Sample Answers for Activity Pages

Day 1	See "Model the Skill" below.
Day 2	Read aloud the title and directions. Have students cut out pictures at the bottom and paste the ones with the **/ôr/** sound in the boxes around the horse. (**horn, fork, corn, door, torch, stork**)
Day 3	Read aloud the title and directions. Have students find one word in each sentence with the variant vowel **/ôr/**. Then have them write the letters that make the vowel sound. (**corn/or; horn/or; door/oor; snore/or; floor/oor; boar/oar**)
Day 4	Read aloud the title and directions. Model how to do the first one by reading the word **born**. Then show how to take away **b** and add **h** to make the new word **horn**.
Day 5	Read the directions aloud and have students read the words. Allow time for students to complete the first task. Then pronounce the words **port**, **door**, and **oar** and ask students to write them on the lines. Afterward, meet individually with students to discuss their results. Use their responses to plan further instruction and review.

Model the Skill

◆ Hand out the Day 1 activity page and crayons.

◆ Write the word **store** on the chalkboard. **Say:** *Today you are going to blend words that have the variant vowel **/ôr/**. You will blend the sounds to read words. Look at the word **store**. Put your finger under the letter **s** at the beginning of the word and say the sounds aloud with me, moving your finger as we reach each letter sound.* Model how to blend the sounds. Put your finger under each letter as you extend the sound that each letter stands for. **Say: /s/ /t/ /ôr/.**

◆ **Say:** *What vowel sound do you hear in **store**? Listen again: **/s/ /t/ /ôr/**. The vowel sound is not long or short. It is not the vowel sound you hear in **star** or **girl**. It is a different vowel sound. The letters **or**, **oor**, and **oar** stand for the **/ôr/** vowel sound.*

◆ Direct students to the activity page. Have them find and color the pictures that make the **/ôr/** sound. Write the words on the board as they find them: **door**, **corn**, and **pork**. Read each word slowly, circling the letters that make the **/ôr/** sound.

◆ Point out actions that have the variant vowel **/ôr/** sound in their name. Write a few on chart paper and read aloud the words.

Sound Search: Variant Vowel /ôr/

soar

roar

tore

snore

force

wore

Name _____

At the Store

Color the things you see that have an /or/ sound like store.

Unit 10 • Everyday Phonics Intervention Activities Grade 3 • ©2010 Newmark Learning, LLC

Sounds Like Horse

Cut out the pictures and paste the ones that have the same vowel sound as *horse* in the boxes.

Find a Vowel

Find one word in each sentence with the variant vowel **/ôr/**. Circle the word and write the letters that stand for the **/ôr/** sound.

 I eat corn.

 I blow a horn.

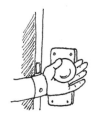 Shut the door!

 We snore.

 The floor is wet.

 It is a wild boar! _____

Unit 10 • Everyday Phonics Intervention Activities Grade 3 • ©2010 Newmark Learning, LLC

Sound Switch-Around

Read the word. Subtract a letter or letters and add a new letter or letters to make a new word. Then read the new word.

born	– b + h =	
tore	– t + w =	
door	– d + fl =	
roar	– r + s =	
pork	– p + st =	
fort	– f + sh =	
porch	– p + t =	
snore	– sn + sc =	
thorn	– th + w =	

Name _____

Assessment

Read the words. Circle the ones that have the same vowel sound as *born*.

floor	sort
score	hurt
park	door
more	board
turn	

Listen to your teacher say each word. Write the words on the lines.

1. _____

2. _____

3. _____

Overview   r-Controlled Digraphs

Directions and Sample Answers for Activity Pages

Day 1	See "Model the Skill" below.
Day 2	Read aloud the title and directions. Invite students to name each picture clue, explaining that each one includes the **/r/** sound. Then help students complete the crossword by filling in the words. (**Across:** 2. spear; 4. tear; 5. deer. **Down:** 1. beard; 3. ear.)
Day 3	Read aloud the title and directions. Have students circle one or more words in each sentence that has the **/r/** sound. Then have them write the letters that make that sound. (1. **steer/eer.** 2. **beard/ear.** 3. **hear/ear; ear/ear.** 4. **cheer/eer.** 5. **deer/eer.**)
Day 4	Read aloud the title and directions. Model how to do the first one by reading the word **fear**. Then show how to take away **f** and add **y** to make the new word **year**.
Day 5	Read the directions aloud and have students read the words. Allow time for students to complete the first task. Then pronounce the words **peer**, **gear**, **steer**, and **smear** and ask students to write them on the lines. Afterward, meet individually with students to discuss their results. Use their responses to plan further instruction and review.

Model the Skill

◆ Hand out the Day 1 activity page.

◆ Direct students' attention to the picture of the deer, and write **deer** on the board. **Say:** *This is a picture of a deer. Listen for the vowel sound as I say the word again: /d/ /ē/ /r/.* The vowel sound is the long **e** sound followed by an **/r/** sound. Explain that the letters **eer** and **ear** both have an **r**-controlled vowel sound.

◆ Help students find other pictures that have an **r**-controlled vowel sound and draw a line from those pictures to the deer in the middle. Write the words on the board as you find them: **ear**, **tear**, and **steer**. Read each word slowly, circling the letters that have an **r**-controlled vowel sound in each word. Give students time to draw a line connecting those words to the deer.

◆ Point out actions that have an **r**-controlled vowel sound. Write a few on chart paper and read aloud the words.

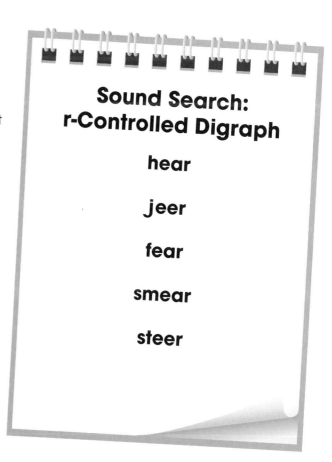

Sound Search:
r-Controlled Digraph

hear

jeer

fear

smear

steer

Sounds Like Ear

Color the things you see that have an r-controlled sound like *ear*.

 Unit 11 • Everyday Phonics Intervention Activities Grade 3 • ©2010 Newmark Learning, LLC

Crossword Puzzle

Say the name of each picture. Then write each picture name in the puzzle.

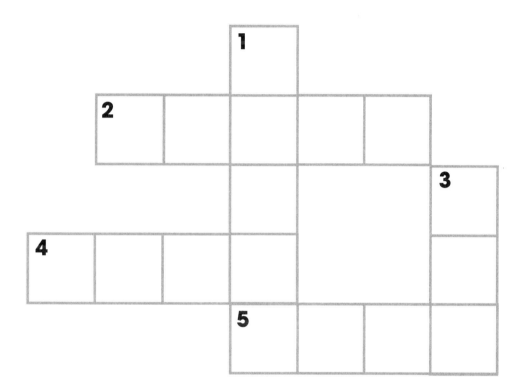

Across   ## Down

2    **1**

4    **3**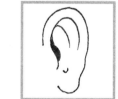

5

Find a Vowel

Find one or more words in each sentence with the /r/ sound. Circle the words and write the letters that stand for the /r/ sound.

 Steer the car. _____

 His beard is long. _____

 I hear with my ear. _____

 We cheer! _____

 The deer is big. _____

Unit 11 • Everyday Phonics Intervention Activities Grade 3 • ©2010 Newmark Learning, LLC

Make a Word

Read the word. Subtract a letter or letters and add a new letter or letters to make a new word. Then read the new word.

fear	– f + y =	
veer	– v + p =	
near	– n + h =	
cheer	– ch + sh =	
tear	– t + d =	
deer	– d + st =	
spear	– sp + cl =	
steer	– st + sn =	

Assessment

Read the words. Circle the ones that have an /r/ sound.

park   curl

fear   year

dirt   fur

near   sneer

peer   beard

Listen to your teacher say each word. Write the words on the lines.

1. _____   3. _____

2. _____   4. _____

Overview Variant Vowel /âr/

Directions and Sample Answers for Activity Pages

Day 1	See "Model the Skill" below.
Day 2	Read aloud the title and directions. Invite students to name each picture. Then ask students to circle and write the words that name the pictures. (**stair, pear, hare, bear**)
Day 3	Read aloud the title and directions. Have students read each clue and the two answers. Then have them circle the correct answer. (1. **chair.** 2. **pear.** 3. **hair.** 4. **square.** 5. **stair.** 6. **fare.**)
Day 4	Read aloud the title and directions. Model how to do the first one by reading the word **pair**. Then show how to take away **p** and add **f** to make the new word **fair**.
Day 5	Read the directions aloud and have students read the words. Allow time for students to complete the first task. Then pronounce the words **air, dare,** and **wear** and ask students to write them on the lines. Afterward, meet individually with students to discuss their results. Use their responses to plan further instruction and review.

Model the Skill

◆ Hand out the Day 1 activity page and crayons.

◆ Write the word **care** on the board. **Say:** *What vowel sound do you hear in the word* **care***? Listen again: /c/ /âr/. The vowel sound is not long or short. It is not the vowel sound you hear in* **star, girl, corn,** *or* **deer***. It is a different vowel sound.* Now write the words **air** and **wear** and say them aloud. Explain that each of these words has the same vowel sound as **care**—the letters **air, are,** and **ear** stand for the /âr/ vowel sound.

◆ Direct students to the activity page. Have them find and color the pictures that make the /âr/ sound. Write the words on the board as they find them: **bear, chair,** and **square**. Read each word slowly, circling the letters that make the /âr/ sound.

◆ Point out items in the school that have the variant vowel /âr/ sound. Write a few on chart paper and read aloud the words.

Sound Search: Variant Vowel /âr/

chair

air

hair

pair

square

stair

Bear in Chair

Color the things you see that have an /ar/ sound like *air*.

Picture I.D.

Circle and write the word that names each picture.

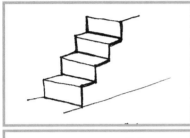

stair stare _____

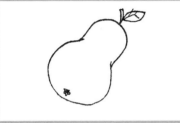

pair pear _____

hair hare _____

bear bare _____

Riddle Fun

Circle the word that solves the riddle.

1. You sit on it.   chair   cheer

2. You eat it.   park   pear

3. You brush it.   hair   hard

4. It is a shape.   square   squish

5. You climb it.   star   stair

6. You pay it.   far   fare

Sound Switch-Around

Read the word. Subtract a letter or letters and add a new letter or letters to make a new word. Then read the new word.

pair	– p + f =	
dare	– d + m =	
bear	– b + sw =	
flair	– fl + ch =	
scare	– sc + gl =	
wear	– w + p =	
blare	– bl + squ =	
fair	– f + st =	

Assessment

Read the words. Circle the ones that have the same vowel sound as *fair*.

care   wear

swear   hair

farm   stare

rare   far

fear

Listen to your teacher say each word. Write the words on the lines.

1. _____

2. _____

3. _____

Overview Variant Vowel /o͞o/

Directions and Sample Answers for Activity Pages

Day 1	See "Model the Skill" below.
Day 2	Read aloud the title and directions. Invite students to name each picture. Then have them cut out the pictures and paste ones that have the same vowel sound as **tool** around the toolbox. (**screwdriver, boot, glue, cube, moon, broom**)
Day 3	Read aloud the title and directions. Invite students to name each picture clue, explaining that each one includes the variant vowel /o͞o/. Then have students complete the crossword by filling in the words. (**Across:** 3. spoon; 5. flute. **Down:** 1. moon; 2. goose; 3. screw; 4. glue.)
Day 4	Read aloud the title and directions. Model how to do the first one by reading the word **dew**. Then show how to take away **d** and add **n** to make the new word **new**.
Day 5	Read the directions aloud and have students read the words. Allow time for students to complete the first task. Then pronounce the words **noon, clue, dune, few,** and **shoe** and ask students to write them on the lines. Afterward, meet individually with students to discuss their results. Use their responses to plan further instruction and review.

Model the Skill

◆ Hand out the Day 1 activity page and crayons.

◆ Write the words **chew** and **food** on the chalkboard. **Say:** *We chew our food. The words* **chew** *and* **food** *have the same vowel sound. Listen to the vowel sound as I blend the words: /ch/ /o͞o/, /f/ /o͞o/ /d/. The vowel sound /o͞o/ is not long or short. It is not a vowel-**r** sound. It is a different vowel sound. Listen again to the vowel sound: /ch/ /o͞o/, /f/ /o͞o/ /d/.*

◆ Point to the word **chew** on the board and explain that in this word, the letters **ew** stand for the /o͞o/ sound. Then point to the word **food** and explain that in this word, the letters **oo** stand for the /o͞o/ sound. Explain that the letters **ue**, as in **blue**, stand for the /o͞o/, too, as well as **u** when followed by a consonant and silent **e**, as in **flute**.

◆ Have students find and color pictures that make the /o͞o/ sound. Write the words on the board as they find them: **pool, tube, shoe,** and **Sue**. Read each word slowly, circling the letters that make the /o͞o/ sound in each word: **oo, ube, oe, ue**.

◆ List words we use to describe things, such as clothing or people, that have the variant vowel /o͞o/ sound. Write a few on chart paper and read aloud the words. Invite students to add to the list.

**Sound Search:
Variant Vowel /o͞o/**

new

blue

cool

droopy

loose

rude

cute

Cool Pool

Color the things you see that have an **/o͞o/** sound like *tool*.

Name _____

Into the Toolbox

Cut out the pictures and paste the ones that have the same vowel sound as *tool* around the toolbox.

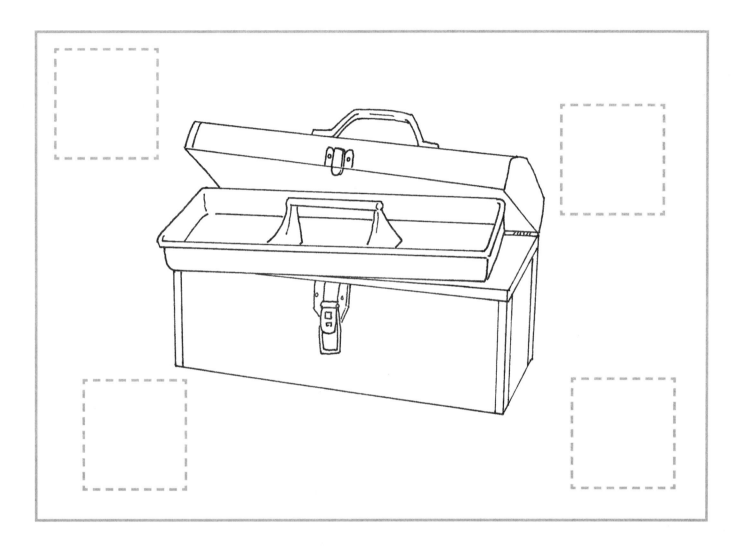

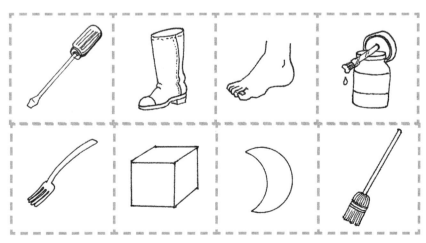

Crossword Puzzle

Say the name of each clue. Then write each name in the puzzle.

Across

3

5

Down

1

2

3

4

Unit 13 • Everyday Phonics Intervention Activities Grade 3 • ©2010 Newmark Learning, LLC

Name _____

Sound Switch-Around

Read the word. Subtract a letter or letters and add a new letter or letters to make a new word. Then read the new word.

dew	– d + n =	
zoo	– z + t =	
tube	– e + c =	
true	– tr + bl =	
room	– r + gl =	
chew	– ch + gr =	
tooth	– t + b =	
stool	– st + dr =	
group	– gr + s =	
troop	– tr + sc =	

Assessment

Read the words. Circle the ones that have the same vowel sound as *moose.*

flew	snow
rude	tube
mouse	mask
prune	new
stoop	duke

Listen to your teacher say each word. Write the words on the lines.

1. _____

2. _____

3. _____

4. _____

5. _____

Unit 13 • Everyday Phonics Intervention Activities Grade 3 • ©2010 Newmark Learning, LLC

Overview Variant Vowel /ô/

Directions and Sample Answers for Activity Pages

Day 1	See "Model the Skill" below.
Day 2	Read aloud the title and directions. Invite students to name each picture. Then ask students to circle and write the word that names the picture. (**ball, walk, claw, saw, cloth, salt**)
Day 3	Read aloud the title and directions. Have students draw a line under the words in each row that have the same **/ô/** vowel sound as the first word in the row. (**walk, lost; fought, law; fault, gloss; chalk, taught; small, yawn; wall, long**)
Day 4	Read aloud the title and directions. Model how to do the first one by reading the word **tall**. Then show how to take away **t** and add **h** to make the new word **hall**.
Day 5	Read the directions aloud and have students read the words. Allow time for students to complete the first task. Then pronounce the words **call, fault, hawk, lost, caught,** and **thought** and ask students to write them on the lines. Afterward, meet individually with students to discuss their results. Use their responses to plan further instruction and review.

Model the Skill

◆ Hand out the Day 1 activity page and crayons.

◆ Write the following words on the chalkboard: **walk, dawn, haunt, cost, taught,** and **bought. Say:** *We walk at dawn. The words **walk** and **dawn** have the same vowel sound. Listen to the vowel sound as I blend the words: /w/ /ô/ /k/, /d/ /ô/ /n/. The vowel sound /ô/ is not long or short. It is a different vowel sound. Listen again to the vowel sound: /w/ /ô/ /k/, /d/ /ô/ /n/.*

◆ Point to the word **walk** on the board and explain that in this word, the letters **al** stand for the **/ô/** sound. Then point to the word **dawn** and explain that in this word, the letters **aw** stand for the **/ô/** sound. Point to the rest of the words on the board, explaining that each has the **/ô/** sound. Blend each word, circling the letters that stand for the **/ô/** sound (**au** in **haunt**, **o** in **cost**, **augh** in **taught**, **ough** in **bought**).

◆ Have students find and color pictures that make the **/ô/** sound. Write the words on the board as they find them: **ball, toss, walk,** and **straw**. Read each word slowly, circling the letters that make the **/ô/** sound in each word: **al, o, al, al, aw**.

◆ List action words that have the variant vowel **/ô/** sound. Write a few on chart paper and read aloud the words. Invite students to add to the list.

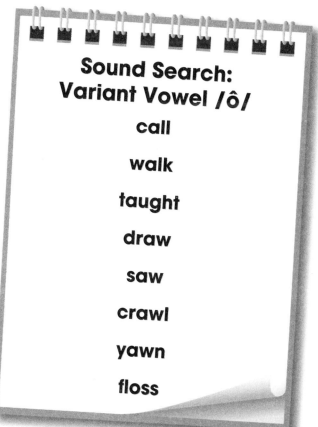

**Sound Search:
Variant Vowel /ô/**

call

walk

taught

draw

saw

crawl

yawn

floss

Name _____

Have a Ball

Color the things you see that have an /ô/ sound like *walk*.

Unit 14 • Everyday Phonics Intervention Activities Grade 3 • ©2010 Newmark Learning, LLC

Picture I.D.

Circle and write the word that names each picture.

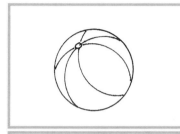 bowl ball_____

 walk wake_____

 claw clue_____

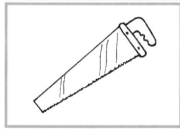 sew saw_____

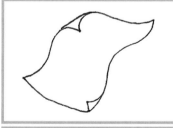 cloth clot_____

 sat salt_____

Same Sounds

Underline words in each row that have the same vowel sound as the word at the beginning of the row.

raw	rat	walk	lost
song	fought	law	soup
fall	fault	fail	gloss
bought	boat	chalk	taught
vault	small	vote	yawn
caught	wall	long	catch

Unit 14 • Everyday Phonics Intervention Activities Grade 3 • ©2010 Newmark Learning, LLC

Name _____

Sound Switch-Around

Read the word. Subtract a letter or letters and add a new letter or letters to make a new word. Then read the new word.

tall	– t + h =	
stalk	– st + ch =	
caught	– c + t =	
bought	– b + s =	
haunt	– h + t =	
fault	– f + v =	
jaw	– j + cl =	
broth	– br + cl =	

Assessment

Read the words. Circle the ones that have the same vowel sound as *frost***.**

tall   lost

moth   salt

frown   feast

lawn   song

fast   ought

Listen to your teacher say each word. Write the words on the lines.

1. _____   4. _____

2. _____   5. _____

3. _____   6. _____

UNIT 15

Overview Variant Vowel /o͝o/

Directions and Sample Answers for Activity Pages

Day 1	See "Model the Skill" below.
Day 2	Read aloud the title and directions. Invite students to name each picture clue, explaining that each one includes the /o͝o/ sound. Then have students complete the crossword by filling in the words. (**Across:** 2. hood; 4. cookie. **Down:** 1. foot; 2. hook; 3. book.)
Day 3	Read aloud the title and directions. Have students read the words in each row and then circle the two that rhyme. (1. **full/wool**. 2. **hood/would**. 3. **foot/put**. 4. **should/good**. 5. **pull/bull**. 6. **could/stood**.)
Day 4	Read aloud the title and directions. Model how to do the first one by reading the word **wood**. Then show how to take away **w** and add **h** to make the new word **hood**.
Day 5	Read the directions aloud and have students read the words. Allow time for students to complete the first task. Then pronounce the words **took**, **should**, and **full** and ask students to write them on the lines. Afterward, meet individually with students to discuss their results. Use their responses to plan further instruction and review.

Model the Skill

◆ Hand out the Day 1 activity page and crayons.

◆ Write the word **shook** on the board. **Say:** *What vowel sound do you hear in the word* **shook***? Listen again: /sh/ /o͝o/ /k/. The vowel sound is not long or short. It is not a vowel-r sound. It is a different vowel sound.* Point out that the letters **oo** stand for the /o͝o/ sound. Now write and say the words **pull** and **could**. Point out that these words have the same vowel sound as **shook**. Explain that in these words, the letters **u** (in **pull**) and **oul** (in **could**) stand for the same /o͝o/ sound.

◆ Direct students to the activity page. Have them find and color the pictures that make the /o͝o/ sound. Write the words on the board as they find them: **push, foot, brook, bush**. Read each word slowly, circling the letters that make the /o͝o/ sound.

◆ Point out actions that have the variant vowel /o͝o/ sound in their names. Write a few on chart paper and read aloud the words.

**Sound Search:
Variant Vowel /o͝o/**

cook

look

shook

stood

pull

push

Swinging by the Brook

Color the things you see that have an /ŏŏ/ sound like *book*.

Crossword Puzzle

Say the name of each picture. Then write each picture name in the puzzle.

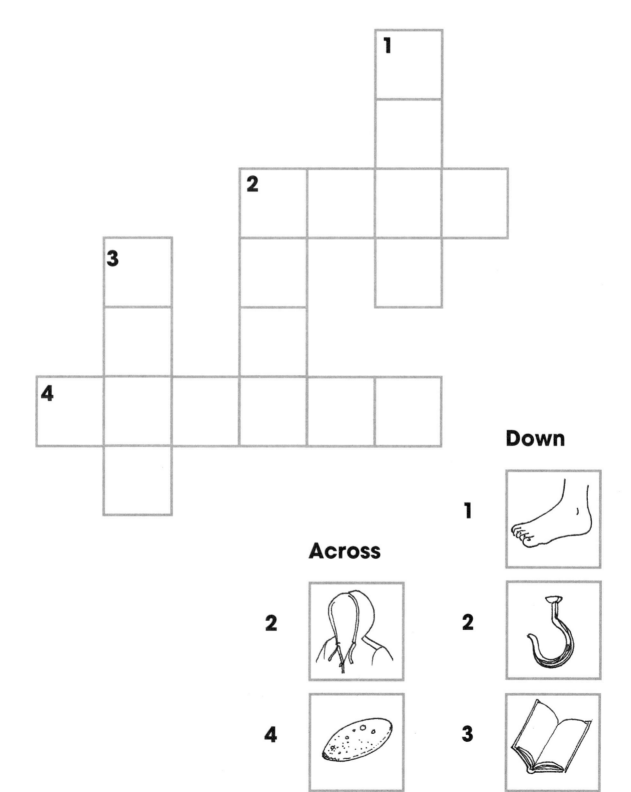

Down

Across

Rhyme Time

Circle the two words in each row that rhyme.

1. full   wool   peel

2. hole   hood   would

3. foot   put   pet

4. should   shop   good

5. bell   pull   bull

6. could   stood   cod

Sound Switch-Around

Read the word. Subtract a letter or letters and add a new letter or letters to make a new word. Then read the new word.

wood	– w + h =	
push	– p + b =	
took	– t + n =	
could	– c + w =	
stood	– st + g =	
crook	– cr + sh =	

Assessment

Read the words. Circle the ones that have the same vowel sound as *full*.

bush   look

good   fun

could   hoof

fill   fuss

pull

Listen to your teacher say each word. Write the words on the lines.

1. _____

2. _____

3. _____

Overview   Diphthong /ou/

Directions and Sample Answers for Activity Pages

Day 1	See "Model the Skill" below.
Day 2	Read aloud the title and directions. Have students cut out pictures at the bottom and paste the ones with the **/ou/** sound around the cloud. (**crown, house, owl, cow, couch**)
Day 3	Read aloud the title and directions. Have students read each clue and the two answers. Then have them circle the correct answer. (1. **owl**. 2. **cloud**. 3. **crown**. 4. **gown**. 5. **couch**. 6. **out**.)
Day 4	Read aloud the title and directions. Invite students to read the sentences and circle one or more words in each sentence with the **/ou/** sound. Have them write the letters that stand for **/ou/**. (1. **cow/ow**. 2. **counts/ou**. 3. **sound/ou**. 4. **mouse/ou**. 5. **bow/ow**. 6. **loud/ou**. 7. **sprouts/ou**. 8. **down/ow**.)
Day 5	Read the directions aloud and have students read the words. Allow time for students to complete the first task. Then pronounce the words **bounce**, **count**, **now**, and **prowl** and ask students to write them on the lines. Afterward, meet individually with students to discuss their results. Use their responses to plan further instruction and review.

Model the Skill

◆ Hand out the Day 1 activity page and crayons.

◆ Write the words **south** and **town** on the chalkboard. **Say:** *We live south of town. The words* **south** *and* **town** *have the same vowel sound. Listen to the vowel sound as I blend the words:* **/s/ /ou/ /th/, /t/ /ou/ /n/**. *The vowel sound* **/ou/** *is not long or short. It is not a vowel-***r** *sound. It is a different vowel sound. Listen again to the vowel sound:* **/s/ /ou/ /th/, /t/ /ou/ /n/**.

◆ Point to the word **south** on the board and explain that in this word, the letters **ou** stand for the **/ou/** sound. Then point to the word **town** and explain that in this word, the letters **ow** stand for the **/ou/** sound.

◆ Have students find and color pictures that make the **/ou/** sound. Write the words on the board as they find them: **clown, frown, cloud,** and **mouse**. Read each word slowly, circling the letters that make the **/ou/** sound in each word.

◆ List animals, animal sounds, and animal movements that have the diphthong **/ou/**. Write them on chart paper and read aloud.

**Sound Search:
Diphthong /ou/**

cow	**howl**
fowl	**bound**
sow	**pounce**
trout	**bounce**
owl	**crouch**
growl	**prowl**

A Sad Clown

Color the things you see that have an /ou/ sound like _town_.

In the Clouds

Cut out the pictures and paste the ones that have the same vowel sound as *cloud* around the picture of the cloud.

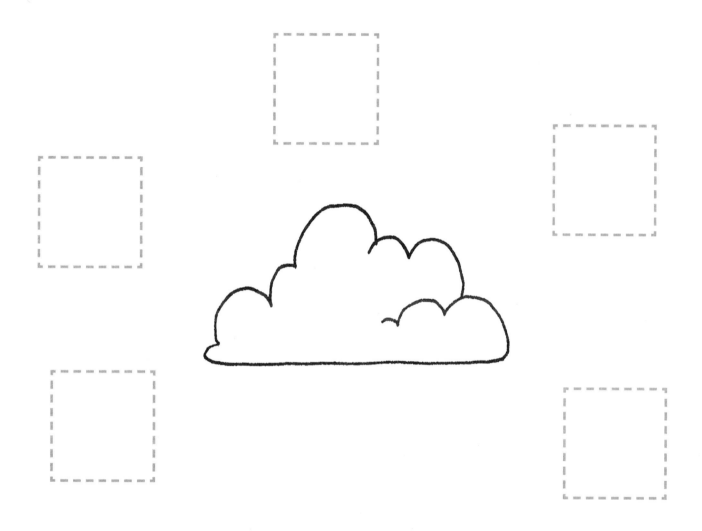

Riddle Fun

Circle the word that solves the riddle.

1. It says, "Who, who."   owl   only

2. It is in the sky.   cold   cloud

3. A king wears one.   cane   crown

4. A queen wears one. gown   goon

5. You sit on it.   coach   couch

6. It is not in.   out   off

Unit 16 • Everyday Phonics Intervention Activities Grade 3 • ©2010 Newmark Learning, LLC

Sound Hunt

Circle the word that has the sound **/ou/** as in *town*. Then write the letters that make that sound on the line.

 The cow says, "Moo." _____

 The kid counts. _____

 Do not make a sound. _____

 The mouse is big. _____

 We bow. _____

 It's too loud! _____

 The plant sprouts. _____

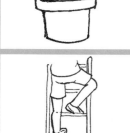 I climb down. _____

Name _____

Assessment

Read the words. Circle the ones that have the same vowel sound as the word *sound*.

loud	snow
rude	chow
vow	mask
proud	blouse
howl	new

Listen to your teacher say each word. Write the words on the lines.

1. _____

2. _____

3. _____

4. _____

Unit 16 • Everyday Phonics Intervention Activities Grade 3 • ©2010 Newmark Learning, LLC

Overview Diphthong /oi/

Directions and Sample Answers for Activity Pages

Day 1	See "Model the Skill" below.
Day 2	Read aloud the title and directions. Have students cut out pictures at the bottom and paste the ones with the **/oi/** sound around the toy box. (**coin, cowboy, oil, soil, boy**)
Day 3	Read aloud the title and directions. Have students find and circle the two words that rhyme in each row. (1. **soy/joy**. 2. **coil/foil**. 3. **join/coin**. 4. **soil/toil**. 5. **moist/hoist**. 6. **enjoy/destroy**.)
Day 4	Read aloud the title and directions. Model how to do the first one by reading the word **joy**. Then show how to take away **j** and add **c** to make the new word **coy**.
Day 5	Read the directions aloud and have students read the words. Allow time for students to complete the first task. Then pronounce the words **joy**, **soil**, **destroy**, and **spoil** and ask students to write them on the lines. Afterward, meet individually with students to discuss their results. Use their responses to plan further instruction and review.

Model the Skill

◆ Hand out the Day 1 activity page and crayons.

◆ Write the words **toy** and **noise** on the chalkboard. **Say:** *That toy makes a lot of noise! The words* **toy** *and* **noise** *have the same vowel sound. Listen to the vowel sound as I blend the words:* **/t/ /oi/**, **/n/ /oi/ /z/**. *The vowel sound* **/oi/** *is not long or short. It is not a vowel-**r** sound. It is a different vowel sound. Listen again to the vowel sound:* **/t/ /oi/**, **/n/ /oi/ /z/**.

◆ Point to the word **toy** on the board and explain that in this word, the letters **oy** stand for the **/oi/** sound. Then point to the word **noise** and explain that in this word, the letters **oi** stand for the **/oi/** sound.

◆ Have students find and color pictures that make the **/oi/** sound. Write the words on the board as they find them: **Roy**, **boy**, and **coin**. Read each word slowly, circling the letters that make the **/oi/** sound in each word.

◆ List action words with the diphthong **/oi/**. Write a few on chart paper and read aloud the words. Invite students to add to the list.

Sound Search:
Diphthong /oi/

boil

spoil

enjoy

join

point

hoist

destroy

Name _____

Collecting Coins

Color the things you see that have an /oi/ sound like boy.

Unit 17 • Everyday Phonics Intervention Activities Grade 3 • ©2010 Newmark Learning, LLC

The Toy Box

Cut out the pictures and paste the ones that have the same vowel sound as *toy* **around the toy box.**

Rhyme Time

Circle the two words in each row that rhyme.

1. soy   joy   job

2. doll   coil   foil

3. join   con   coin

4. sold   soil   toil

5. moist   hoist   more

6. enjoy   angry   destroy

Name _____

Sound Switch-Around

Read the word. Subtract a letter or letters and add a new letter to make a new word. Then read the new word.

joy	– j + c =	
spoil	– sp + f =	
loyal	– l + r =	
broil	– br + t =	
moist	– m + h =	
point	– p + j =	

Assessment

Read the words. Circle the ones that have the same vowel sound as *noise*.

joint	soy
nose	snow
toy	Troy
coil	oil
not	ploy

Listen to your teacher say each word. Write the words on the lines.

1. _____   3. _____

2. _____   4. _____

Overview Soft c, g

Directions and Sample Answers for Activity Pages

Day 1	See "Model the Skill" below.
Day 2	Read aloud the title and directions. Have students cut out pictures at the bottom and paste ones with an **/s/** sound under Alice and ones with a **/j/** sound under George. (**Alice:** circle, fence, cereal, cent, ice. **George:** cage, orange, gingerbread man.)
Day 3	Read aloud the title and directions. Have students underline the word in each row that has the same beginning sound as the first word in the row. (**joke/gem; sat/city; jump/gym; soup/cell; join/germ; sun/cent**)
Day 4	Read aloud the title and directions. Invite students to read the sentences and circle a word in each sentence with a soft **c** or soft **g** sound in it. Have them write the letter that stands for the soft **c** or soft **g**. (**huge/g; mice/c; gym/g; cent/c; ice/c; cage/g; stage/g; pencil/c**)
Day 5	Read the directions aloud and have students read the words. Allow time for students to complete the first task. Then pronounce the words **germ**, **city**, **page**, and **space** and ask students to write them on the lines. Afterward, meet individually with students to discuss their results. Use their responses to plan further instruction and review.

Model the Skill

◆ Hand out the Day 1 activity page.

◆ Write the word **gem** on the board. **Say:** *What a gem! What sound do you hear at the beginning of the word **gem**? Listen again: **/j/ /e/ /m/**. That's right. The **g** makes a **/j/** sound in the word **gem**. When **g** stands for **/j/** (rather than **/g/**), it is called a soft **g**.*

◆ Write the word **ice** on the board and sound it out. Point out that in **ice**, **c** stands for the **/s/** sound. Explain that when **c** stands for **/s/** (rather than **/k/**) it is called soft **c**.

◆ Direct students' attention to the activity page. Have them circle the pictures that have a soft **c** in them. Have them put a square around pictures with a soft **g** sound. Explain that the soft **c** or soft **g** may be at the beginning, middle, or end of the word. Write the words on the board as they find them: **bridge**, **giraffe**, **mice**, **cymbals**, and **dancer**. Have students identify the word as having a soft **c** or soft **g**.

◆ Point out words with a soft **c** or soft **g** sound in them that are used to describe things. Write a few on chart paper and read aloud the words. Invite students to add to the list.

Sound Search: Soft c, g

fancy

peaceful

certain

graceful

huge

giant

generous

Everyone Loves a Parade

Color the things you see that have a soft _c_ sound like _ice_ or a soft _g_ sound like _gem_.

Unit 18 • Everyday Phonics Intervention Activities Grade 3 • ©2010 Newmark Learning, LLC

Name _____

Alice or George

Cut out the pictures and paste the ones that have an */s/* sound under Alice and ones with a */j/* sound under George.

Same Sounds

Underline the word in each row that has the same beginning sound as the word at the beginning of the row.

joke	game	gem
sat	city	cat
jump	gym	gum
soup	cup	cell
join	gone	germ
sun	cent	can

Unit 18 • Everyday Phonics Intervention Activities Grade 3 • ©2010 Newmark Learning, LLC

Search for Soft *c* and *g*

Find a word in each sentence that has a soft *c* or soft *g* sound. Circle the word and write the letter that stands for the sound on the line.

 He is huge! _____

 I see three mice. _____

 I lift at the gym. _____

 I have one cent. _____

 I wear ice skates. _____

 The bird is in a cage. _____

 She sings on stage. _____

 I use a pencil. _____

Name _____

Assessment

Read the words. Circle the ones that end with a soft *c* or soft *g* sound.

ring	age
page	rock
sock	rice
race	face
egg	stage

Listen to your teacher say each word. Write the words on the lines.

1. _____

3. _____

2. _____

4. _____

Overview   Silent Letters

Directions and Sample Answers for Activity Pages

Day 1	See "Model the Skill" below.
Day 2	Read aloud the title and directions. Invite students to name each picture. Then have students circle the two pictures that have the same silent letter. (**knife/knight, write/wrist, lamb/thumb, whistle/castle**)
Day 3	Read aloud the title and directions. Have students name each picture clue, explaining that each one has a silent letter. Then have students complete the crossword puzzle by filling in the words. (**Across:** 3. whisker; 4. knee; 5. comb. **Down:** 1. two; 2. sign; 3. knot.)
Day 4	Read aloud the title and directions. Invite students to read the sentences and circle a word in each sentence that has a silent letter. Have them write the silent letter on the line. (**write/w; climb/b; lick/c; gnat/g; knits/k; ballet/t; wheels/h**)
Day 5	Read the directions aloud and name the pictures together. Allow time for students to complete the first task. Then pronounce the words **wheat**, **wrong**, **crumb**, **gnaw**, **kneel**, and **rack** and ask students to write them on the lines. Afterward, meet individually with students to discuss their results. Use their responses to plan further instruction and review.

Model the Skill

◆ Hand out the Day 1 activity page and crayons.

◆ Write **write** on the board. Point to the letters as you **say:** *We write at school. Listen to the sounds in the word:* **/r/ /ī/ /t/**. *How many sounds do you hear? You hear three sounds. Notice you do not hear the* **/w/** *sound. That's because* **w** *is silent.* **W** *is silent before* **r** *at the beginning of a word.*

◆ Write these words on the board: **climb, listen, rhyme, know,** and **pack**. Point to each word as you **say:** *We do other things in school, too. We* **climb** *at recess. We* **listen** *to our teacher. We* **rhyme** *words. We* **know** *facts. We* **pack** *our books.* Point to each word and circle the silent letter. Explain the rule that generally applies: **climb** (**b** is silent after **m**), **listen** (**t** is silent in words with **-sten** and **-stle**), **rhyme** (**h** is silent when it follows **r** or **k**), **know** (**k** is silent before **n** at the beginning of a word), and **pack** (**c** is silent in the cluster **ck**).

◆ Have students color pictures that have a silent letter. Write the words on the board as they find them: **school, thumb, knee, climb, whispering,** and **sign**. Read each word, circling the silent letter.

◆ List parts of the body with a silent letter. Write them on chart paper and read aloud.

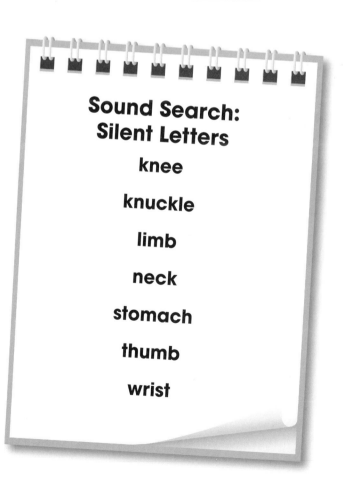

**Sound Search:
Silent Letters**

knee

knuckle

limb

neck

stomach

thumb

wrist

Name _____

School Days

Color the things you see that have silent letters like the word *write*.

Silent Letter I.D.

Circle the two pictures in each row that have the same silent letter. Then write the silent letter on the line.

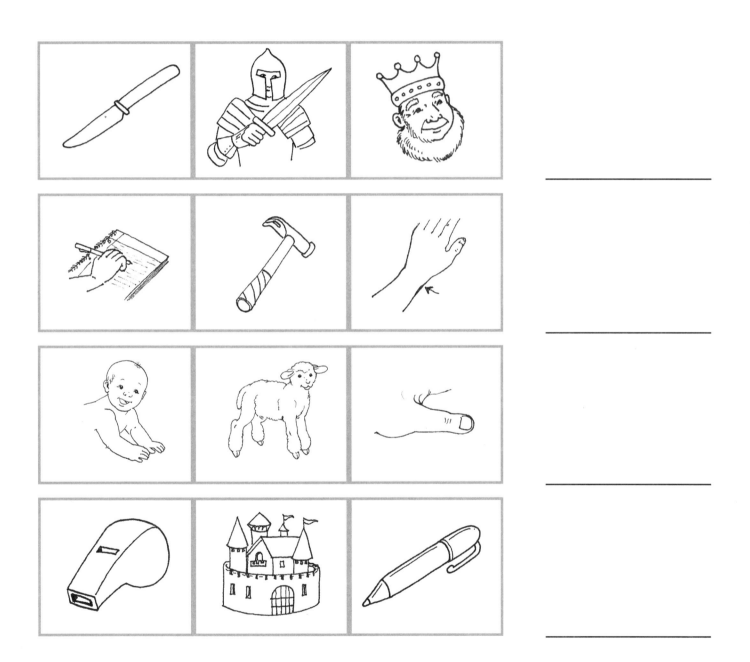

Crossword Puzzle

Say the name of each clue. Then write each name in the puzzle.

Across

3

4

5

Down

1

2

4

Unit 19 • Everyday Phonics Intervention Activities Grade 3 • ©2010 Newmark Learning, LLC

Search for Silent Letters

Find a word in each sentence that has a silent letter. Circle the word and write the silent letter on the line.

 I write notes.

 Climb the tree.

 I lick a lollipop.

 Hit the gnat.

 My mom knits.

 I like ballet.

 Our wagon has wheels. _____

Assessment

Read the words. Circle the ones that have a silent letter.

whole   numb

rest   gnarl

whale   sing

wish   knob

soften   sack

Listen to your teacher say each word. Write the words on the lines.

1. _____   4. _____

2. _____   5. _____

3. _____   6. _____

Overview Closed Syllable Pattern

Directions and Sample Answers for Activity Pages

Day 1	See "Model the Skill" below.
Day 2	Read the title and directions aloud. Invite students to divide each word into syllables using the closed syllable pattern. (**bas/ket, cat/nip, traf/fic, sub/tract, hic/cup**) Have students read each word.
Day 3	Read the title and directions aloud. Invite students to sort words into two groups using the closed syllable pattern: double consonants and different consonants. (double consonants: **can/not, at/tract, rab/bit**; different consonants: **hec/tic, cac/tus, sel/dom**) Have students read each word.
Day 4	Read the title and directions aloud. Invite students to locate the six closed syllable words in the story, divide the words into syllables, and read each word to a partner. Assist students who need help dividing the words. (**pic/nic, but/ter, fab/ric, ten/nis, sun/set, con/tent**)
Day 5	Read the directions aloud. Allow time for students to complete the first task. (**bul/let, hus/band, ex/pand, sub/ject**) Next, pronounce the words **jacket**, **cannot**, and **picnic** and ask students to write them on the lines. Afterward, meet individually with students. Ask them to read each word on the assessment page. Discuss their results. Use their responses to plan further instruction and review.

Model the Skill

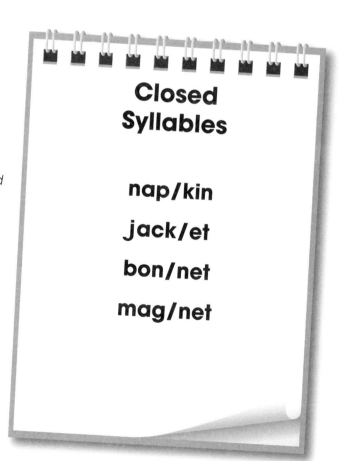

◆ Hand out the Day 1 activity page. Write the word **nap** on the board. Point out that it has one short vowel sound. Have students say the word. **Ask:** *Does this word end with a vowel or a consonant? A consonant. This is an example of a closed syllable.*

◆ **Say:** *You can use what you know about vowel patterns and closed syllables to read longer words. Write the word **napkin** on the first blank of your activity page and follow along as I explain how to divide this word into syllables.* Write the word **napkin** on the board. *First, I circle the two vowels. There are two consonants between the vowels, so I can divide the word between them: **nap/kin**. Copy what I did on your paper.*

◆ Point out that both syllables end with consonants and have a single vowel, so they are both closed syllables. **Say:** *Now I want to read this word. Since vowel sounds in closed syllables are often short, I'll try the short sounds first: **/nap/ /kin/, napkin**.*

◆ Repeat with **jacket (jack/et)**. Explain that **c** and **k** together make the consonant digraph that stands for the **/k/** sound. Explain that you don't divide consonant digraphs.

◆ Then repeat with **bonnet (bon/net)**, **magnet (mag/net)**.

Closed Syllables

nap/kin

jack/et

bon/net

mag/net

Closed Syllable Words

Listen to the example. Read each word aloud. Then divide each word into syllables.

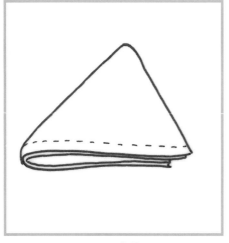

napkin

_____

jacket

_____

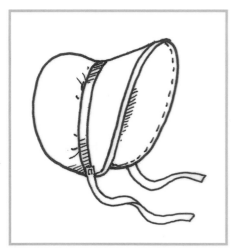

bonnet

_____

magnet

_____

Words Divided

Look at the following words. Divide each word into two closed syllables. Remember the double letter rule. Then read the words to a partner.

Word List:

| basket | catnip | traffic | subtract | hiccup |

_____

_____

_____

_____

_____

Name _____

Closed Syllable Sort

Sort the following words into two groups using a closed syllable pattern: double consonants or different consonants. Share your results with a partner.

Word List

hectic	cactus	seldom
cannot	attract	rabbit

Double Consonants	Different Consonants

The Picnic

Read the story. Locate the six closed syllable words and write them at the bottom of the page. Divide the words into syllables. Read each word to a partner.

Lisa wanted to go to the park and have a picnic. Her aunt said that was a good idea, so they packed lunch. They packed bread and butter, hard-boiled eggs, fruit, and milk. When they got to the park, they laid a large piece of fabric on the ground. After eating lunch, Lisa and her aunt played tennis. They stayed at the park until sunset. Lisa was very content with her day.

1. _____

2. _____

3. _____

4. _____

5. _____

6. _____

Name _____

Assessment

Divide the following words into closed syllables.

| bullet | husband | expand | subject |

_____

_____

_____

_____

Listen to your teacher say each word. Write the words on the lines.

1. _____

2. _____

3. _____

Unit 20 • Everyday Phonics Intervention Activities Grade 3 • ©2010 Newmark Learning, LLC

Overview VCe Syllable Pattern

Directions and Sample Answers for Activity Pages

Day 1	See "Model the Skill" below.
Day 2	Read the title and directions aloud. Invite students to divide each word into syllables using the closed and VCe syllable patterns. (**ex/pose, mis/take, in/side, sup/pose, ac/cuse, col/lide, frus/trate, con/crete, ex/plore**) Have students read each word and choose three words to use in sentences.
Day 3	Read the title and directions aloud. Invite students to sort words into three groups using the VCe syllable pattern: double consonants, different consonants, and consonant blends. (double consonants: **op/pose, sap/phire, im/mune**; different consonants: **ex/cuse, com/bine, rep/tile**; consonant blends: **com/plete, cy/clone, in/flate**) Have students read each word.
Day 4	Read the title and directions aloud. Invite students to unscramble the letters in the VCe words and match them to the correct sentences. (**excite, fuse, drape, twine, exhale, episode, plume, slope**)
Day 5	Read the directions aloud. Allow time for students to complete the first task. (**dif/fuse, mem/brane, ig/nite, en/trap, ef/face, in/sane**) Next, pronounce the words **reptile, commode,** and **explore** and ask students to write them on the lines. Afterward, meet individually with students. Ask them to read each word on the assessment page. Discuss their results. Use their responses to plan further instruction and review.

Model the Skill

◆ Hand out the Day 1 activity page. Write **pole** on the board and read it aloud. Model blending the onset and rime: **/pol/, pole. Say:** *Notice that this word has one syllable, one vowel sound, and a VCe pattern. You can use what you know about vowel patterns and syllables to read longer words.*

◆ Write **tadpole** on the board. **Say:** *Notice the silent final **e** and the other two vowels in this word.* Circle the vowels **a** and **o**. **Ask:** *How many consonants do you see between these two vowels? I will try dividing the word between the two consonants: **tad/pole**.* Point out that the first syllable is a closed syllable and the second syllable has a VCe pattern.

◆ **Say:** *Now I want to read this word. Since vowel sounds in closed syllables are often short, I'll try the short sound for the first syllable. Since vowel sounds in VCe patterns are often long, I'll try the long vowel sound for the second syllable.* Model reading the two parts of the word and blending them together: **/tad/ /pol/, tadpole.**

◆ Repeat with **commode** (**com/mode**) and **explode** (**ex/plode**).

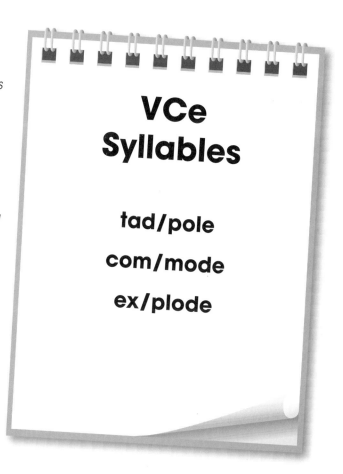

VCe Syllables

tad/pole

com/mode

ex/plode

VCe Syllables

Listen to the example. Read each word aloud. Then divide each word into two syllables.

tadpole

_____

commode

_____

explode

_____

Words Divided

Look at the following words. Divide each word into two syllables. Remember that one syllable is closed and the other syllable has a VCe pattern. Then read the words to a partner.

List 1:	List 2:	List 3:
expose	suppose	frustrate
mistake	accuse	concrete
inside	collide	explore

Choose one word from each list to use in a sentence.

1. _____

   _____

2. _____

   _____

3. _____

   _____

VCe Syllable Sort

Sort the following words into three groups using a VCe syllable pattern: double consonants, different consonants, or consonant blends. Share your results with a partner.

Word List

complete	oppose	excuse
combine	reptile	cyclone
inflate	sapphire	immune

Double Consonants	Different Consonants	Consonant Blends

Unit 21 • Everyday Phonics Intervention Activities Grade 3 • ©2010 Newmark Learning, LLC

VCe Word Scramble

Unscramble the VCe words and write them in the blank in the correct sentence.

xalhee	**cteixe**	**plseo**	**uesf**
praed	**wetni**	**speidoe**	**uepml**

It's almost time for bed, so don't _____ yourself.

If the lights go out, check the _____ box.

_____ this blanket over your shoulders. You look like you are cold.

You can use _____, or rope, to close that box.

Take a deep breath and inhale. Let the breath out while you _____.

My mom let me watch the latest _____ of *Superman* on TV.

That clown looks so funny with that ostrich _____ in his hat.

Don't fall down the _____. It's a long way to the bottom.

Name _____

Assessment

Divide the following words into closed and VCe syllable patterns.

| diffuse | membrane | ignite | entrap | efface | insane |

Listen to your teacher say each word. Write the words on the lines.

1. _____

2. _____

3. _____

Unit 21 • Everyday Phonics Intervention Activities Grade 3 • ©2010 Newmark Learning, LLC

Overview Open Syllable Pattern

Directions and Sample Answers for Activity Pages

Day 1	See "Model the Skill" below.
Day 2	Read the title and directions aloud. Have students read each word. Then invite students to divide each word into syllables using the open syllable pattern. (**ro/dent, hu/man, u/nit, a/gent, so/lo, e/go, cra/zy, ti/dy**) Then have students choose three words to use in a sentence.
Day 3	Read the title and directions aloud. Invite students to sort words into two groups: open/closed syllable patterns and open/open syllable patterns. (open/closed: **robot, siren, silent, totem**; open/open: **shaky, silo, lazy, halo**) Have students share results with a partner.
Day 4	Read the title and directions aloud. Invite students to divide the words into open and closed syllables. Then have students locate the words in the word search. (**so/lid, rhi/no, ru/by, hu/mid, o/pen, fo/cus**)
Day 5	Read the directions aloud. Allow time for students to complete the first task. (**mo/ment, i/tem, pho/to, to/tal, ba/by**) Next, pronounce the words **unit**, **solo**, and **lazy** and ask students to write them on the lines. Afterward, meet individually with students. Ask them to read each word on the assessment page. Discuss their results. Use their responses to plan further instruction and review.

Model the Skill

◆ Hand out the Day 1 activity page. Write **go** and **shy** on the board and ask students to say the words. Point out that each word has one vowel sound, so it is a one-syllable word. Then point out that each word ends in a vowel. **Say:** *A syllable that ends in a vowel is an open syllable. You can use what you know about letter patterns and open syllables to read longer words.*

◆ Write **music** on the board. **Say:** *I will circle the two vowels. Notice the single consonant between the two vowels. When there is one consonant, try dividing the word before the consonant:* **mu/sic**. *Copy what I did on your paper.* Point out that the first syllable ends with a vowel, so it is an open syllable.

◆ **Say:** *Now I want to read this word. Since vowel sounds in open syllables are often long, I'll try the long sound first.* Model reading the two parts of the word and blending them together: **/mu/ /sic/, music**. Remind students that **/sic/** is a closed syllable so they should try a short vowel sound for it.

◆ Repeat with the remaining words. Point out that **music** and **program** are made up of open and closed patterns, and **gravy** and **solo** are made of two open patterns (**pro/gram, gra/vy, so/lo**).

Open Syllables

mu/sic

pro/gram

gra/vy

so/lo

Open Syllables

music

_____

program

_____

gravy

_____

solo

_____

Words Divided

Read the following words. Divide each word into two syllables. Remember that some words have only open syllable patterns while other words have open and closed syllable patterns.

List 1:	List 2:
rodent	solo
human	ego
unit	crazy
agent	tidy

Choose three words from the list to use in a sentence.

1. _____

   _____

2. _____

   _____

3. _____

   _____

Syllable Pattern Sort

Sort the following words into two categories: open/closed syllable patterns and open/open syllable patterns. Share your results with a partner.

Word List

robot	silo	lazy	silent
shaky	siren	halo	totem

Open/Closed	Open/Open

Unit 22 • Everyday Phonics Intervention Activities Grade 3 • ©2010 Newmark Learning, LLC

Word Search

Divide the words into open and closed syllables. Then locate the words in the word search.

solid	rhino	ruby	humid	open	focus

s	u	c	o	f	c	s
z	d	i	m	u	h	r
d	o	a	n	x	d	u
r	h	i	n	o	t	b
w	a	z	v	o	b	y
d	i	l	o	s	t	t
e	n	e	p	o	y	s

Assessment

Divide the following words into syllables. Underline each open syllable.

moment	item	photo	total	baby

Listen to your teacher say each word. Write the words on the lines.

1. _____

2. _____

3. _____

Overview Regular and Irregular Plurals

Directions and Sample Answers for Activity Pages

Day 1	See "Model the Skill" below.
Day 2	Read the title and directions aloud. Invite students to look at the singular nouns and write regular plural words for each noun. Have students read each word to a partner. Then have them choose three words and use them in sentences. (**riddles, actors, fields, churches, taxes, dresses, flurries, bullies, armies**)
Day 3	Read the title and directions aloud. Invite students to look at the singular nouns and write irregular plural words for each noun. Have students read each word to a partner. Then have them choose three words and use them in sentences. (**geese, mice, oxen, knives, wives, calves, deer, dozen, sheep**)
Day 4	Read the title and directions aloud. Invite students to locate eight regular and nine irregular plurals in the narrative. Have students read each word to a partner. (regular: **cows, names, cobras, groups, schools, shoals, coats, lizards**; irregular: **jellyfish, fish, fish, herring, oxen, geese, sheep, deer, mice**)
Day 5	Read the directions aloud. Allow time for students to complete the first task. (**bears, axes, cities, women, leaves, moose**) Next, pronounce the words **riddles, taxes, bullies, geese, wolves,** and **sheep** and ask students to write them on the lines. Afterward, meet individually with students. Ask them to read each word on the assessment page. Discuss their results. Use their responses to plan further instruction and review.

Model the Skill

◆ Hand out the Day 1 activity page. Write the words **cake, dish,** and **baby** on the board. Write the letters **s, z, ch, sh, x** in parentheses next to **dish**.

◆ Say: *Plural means more than one thing. We have many ways to make plurals. Look at the words on the board. Most nouns are made plural by simply adding an **-s**, as in* **cake**. *Write* **cakes** *beside* **cake**. *Words ending in* **sh, ch, c,** *and* **x**, *like the word* **dish**, *need an **-es** to make the plural form, like* **dishes**. *Write* **dishes** *beside* **dish**. *For words ending in* **y**, *drop the* **y** *and add **-ies**, like* **baby**— **babies**. *Write* **babies** *beside* **baby**. *Repeat with* **dog, fox,** *and* **berry**. (**dogs, foxes, berries**)

◆ Write the words **child, wolf,** and **fish**. Say: *Some plural words don't follow the* **s, es, ies** *pattern. These plurals are called irregular plurals. Look at* **child**. *It becomes* **children**. *Write* **children** *next to* **child**. *Look at* **wolf**. *We drop the* **f** *and add **-ves**. Write* **wolves** *next to* **wolf**. *Now look at* **fish**. *Some plural words are exactly the same as their singular form. One fish, two fish, not* **fishes**. *Write* **fish** *beside* **fish**. *Since irregular plurals do not follow rules, they must be memorized. Repeat with* **man, loaf,** *and* **moose**. (**men, loaves, moose**)

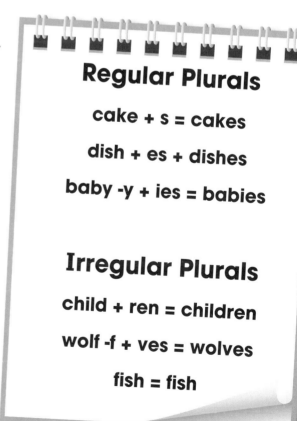

Regular Plurals

cake + s = cakes

dish + es + dishes

baby -y + ies = babies

Irregular Plurals

child + ren = children

wolf -f + ves = wolves

fish = fish

Regular Plurals

 **cake**  _____

 **dish**  _____

 **baby**  _____

1. dog _____   2. fox _____   3. berry _____

Irregular Plurals

 **child**  _____

wolf  _____

fish  _____

1. man _____   2. loaf _____   3. moose _____

Name _____

Follow the Rule

Look at the following singular nouns. For each word, write the regular plural form. Read each plural word to a partner.

List 1:	List 2:	List 3:
riddle _____	church _____	flurry _____
actor _____	tax _____	bully _____
field _____	dress _____	army _____

Choose three words to use in sentences.

1. _____

   _____

2. _____

   _____

3. _____

   _____

Name _____

Remember It!

Look at the following singular nouns. For each word, write the irregular plural form.

List 1:

goose _____

mouse _____

ox _____

List 2:

knife _____

wife _____

calf _____

List 3:

deer _____

dozen _____

sheep _____

Choose three words to use in sentences.

1. _____

_____

2. _____

_____

3. _____

_____

Animal Groups

Read the passage on animal groups. Circle the eight regular plural nouns.
Underline the nine irregular plural nouns. Write them at the bottom of the page.
Read each word to a partner.

You may have heard of a herd of cows. But did you know that almost every animal has a group name?

Some of the names might make you think of the animal, like a quiver of cobras. Some sound plain silly, like a smack of jellyfish.

Groups of fish are called schools. But some fish, like herring, swim in shoals. More than one ox makes a span of oxen. A group of geese is called a gaggle.

You can make many wool coats from a drove of sheep. A few deer make up a herd or a leash. A mouse might join a horde or mischief of mice. Have you ever seen a lounge of lizards?

Regular Plurals	**Irregular Plurals**
1. _____	1. _____
2. _____	2. _____
3. _____	3. _____
4. _____	4. _____
5. _____	5. _____
6. _____	6. _____
7. _____	7. _____
8. _____	8. _____

Assessment

Read the following singular nouns. Write their plurals on the lines provided.

bear   _____

ax   _____

city   _____

woman   _____

leaf   _____

moose   _____

Listen to your teacher say each word. Write the words on the lines.

1. _____

2. _____

3. _____

4. _____

5. _____

6. _____